Strengthening
Refugee Families

Also available from Lyceum Books, Inc.

MODERN SOCIAL WORK THEORY: A CRITICAL INTRO-
DUCTION, 2E, by Malcolm Payne, foreword by Stephen C.
Anderson

CROSS-CULTURAL PRACTICE: SOCIAL WORK WITH
DIVERSE POPULATIONS, by Karen Harper and Jim Lantz

CLINICAL ASSESSMENT FOR SOCIAL WORKERS: QUAN-
TITATIVE AND QUALITATIVE METHODS, by Catheleen
Jordan and Cynthia Franklin

SCHOOL SOCIAL WORK: PRACTICE AND RESEARCH
PERSPECTIVES, 3E, edited by Robert Constable, Shirley
McDonald, and John Flynn

POLICY ANALYSIS AND RESEARCH TECHNOLOGY, by
Thomas Meenaghan and Keith Kilty

STRUCTURING CHANGE: EFFECTIVE PRACTICE FOR
COMMON CLIENT PROBLEMS, edited by Kevin Corcoran

WORKING WITH CHILDREN AND THEIR FAMILIES, by
Martin Herbert, introduction by Charles Zastrow

THE NEW POLITICS OF WELFARE: AN AGENDA FOR
THE 1990s?, edited by Michael McCarthy, preface by Thomas
M. Meenaghan

SOCIAL WORK EDUCATION IN EASTERN EUROPE:
CHANGING HORIZONS, edited by Robert Constable and
Vera Mehta

MARKETING STRATEGIES FOR NONPROFIT ORGANIZA-
TIONS, by Siri Espy

Strengthening Refugee Families

Designing Programs for Refugee and Other Families in Need

Daniel Scheinfeld and
Lorraine B. Wallach
with Trudi Langendorf

LYCEUM
BOOKS, INC.

12 -19 -97

© Lyceum Books, Inc., 1997

Published by

LYCEUM BOOKS, INC.
5758 S. Blackstone Ave.
Chicago, Illinois 60637
773/643-1903 (Fax)
773/643-1902 (Phone)

ISBN 0-925065-13-7

Library of Congress Cataloging-in-Publication Data

Scheinfeld, Daniel, 1933–
    Strengthening refugee families : designing programs for refugee
and other families in need / Daniel Scheinfeld and Lorraine B.
Wallach, with Trudi Langendorf.
        p.   cm.
    Includes bibliographical references.
    ISBN 0-925065-13-7
    1. Refugees—Services for—United States.   2. Family services—
United States.   I. Wallach, Lorraine B.   II. Langendorf, Trudi,
1955–   .   III. Title.
HV640.4.U54S34   1997
362.87′8′0973—dc21
                                                              97-8947
                                                                CIP

Contents

Preface

As refugees from Southeast Asia, Africa, and Eastern Europe resettled in Chicago, social welfare organizations (voluntary agencies, mutual assistance associations, community colleges, and churches) provided services to meet survival needs and to assist refugee families toward self-sufficiency. English as a second language, employment, and adjustment services were emphasized, and adults prioritized as service recipients. A few scattered and short-term programs attempted to address the needs of mothers and young children.

In the mid-1980s, Travelers & Immigrants Aid/Chicago Connections (TIA/CC) led English as a Second Language groups for mothers and preschoolers in our Uptown office. We saw how mothers and children benefited from their interactions with the teachers and each other, but we also learned that because of transportation problems and responsibilities at home, only a few mothers were able to bring their preschoolers to class regularly and that winter weather was a powerful deterrent to attendance. As a result, the program was not reaching the refugee families most in need of assistance.

In 1990, the United Way of Chicago announced a request for proposals through its Family Life Priority Grant program. The guidelines targeted funds for severely underserved communities or populations and newly urgent citywide problems and service needs as identified in the needs assessment process. The potential for three years of funding allowed development of long-term planning. TIA/CC asked Trudi Langendorf to assist in drafting a proposal for comprehensive home-based services to refugee mothers and preschoolers. Trudi Langendorf had been involved with serving Southeast Asian refugees for ten years under the auspices of the Jewish Family and Community Services Resettlement Program and the Refugee Women's Program. As part of her work, she had established and run mother-child groups. Alice Cottingham, TIA/CC's former Director of Program Operations, invited the Erikson Institute to participate, and Lorraine Wallach and Dan Scheinfeld responded. The resulting proposal sought to assure the participation of isolated refugee families through the provision of home-based services. The program involved the entire family in school readiness and school success and built on the relationship between the preschool child and his or her caregiver.

The Refugee Families Program has provided support for over 150 refugee families through eight cycles of instruction since its initial funding in 1990. Under the leadership of TIA/CC's current Chief Operating Officer, Linda Traeger, in 1993 we secured additional funding from the Illinois State Board of Education to provide an Even Start Program. Even Start's emphasis on family literacy is an excellent complement for the Refugee Families Program.

This manual details the program, gives a structure for replication, and, most important, tells the story of families whose lives were changed for the better. The home- and community-based Refugee Families Program began with (and continues under) a simple premise: start where the families *are*—physically, academically, socially, and culturally.

Virginia Koch
Associate Director of Refugee Services
Travelers & Immigrants Aid/Chicago Connections

Acknowledgments

The authors wish to acknowledge the very generous support of United Way of Chicago, Inc., which has made this program possible since its inception in 1991. We also wish to thank the Illinois State Board of Education's Even Start Program, whose support since 1993 has made significant expansion of the program's literacy development facet and bilingual services possible.

The staff of the Heartland Alliance (HA) for Human Needs and Human Rights have provided steadfast support throughout this project. We are particularly grateful to Sid Mohn, Chief Executive Officer, and Linda Traeger, Chief Operating Officer of HA's TIA/CC, for their strong and continuous backing of the program.

Virginia Koch, Associate Director of Refugee Services, has been a major figure in the direction and encouragement of the program since its inception.

Very special thanks go to three sets of people involved in the ongoing implementation and development of the Refugee Families Program and its evaluation: The teachers of the Child-Parent classes, Joanna Amaral, Lisa Bangs, Susan McMillan, and Lisa Rademacher; the bi-lingual counselors, Choulie Hok, Nancy Tran, and Sattha Eap; and the Erikson Institute research assistants, Lori Allen, Mary Pikul, Wendy Soroker, Carrie Thomas, and Jennefer Vaughan.

Principal authors of the respective chapters in this manual are as follows: Daniel Scheinfeld, chapters 1, 6, 9, 10, and 11; Lorraine Wallach, chapters 2, 3, 4, and 5; Lori Allen, chapter 7; Mary Pikul and Lorraine Wallach (with assistance from Nicole Mendyk), chapter 8; Lorraine Wallach and Daniel Scheinfeld, chapter 12; Lorraine Wallach, Appendix A; Lisa Rademacher and Lisa Bangs, with Introduction by Lorraine Wallach, Appendix B; and Daniel Scheinfeld, Appendix D.

Each chapter in the manual draws heavily on interviews with Trudi Langendorf and benefits from her critiques of the ongoing drafts. The writing also is based significantly on the daily reports written by the teachers, the bilingual workers, and Trudi Langendorf over the five years of the program's operation. Additionally, chapters 3, 4, and 5 are based partially on field notes made by research staff.

We wish to convey our deepest gratitude to Catalina Ariza, Brenda Arksey, Becky Baker, Jill Bradley, Diane Brousseau-Pizzi, Dorothy Carpenter, Debbie Hampton, and Nick Wechsler, who read the penultimate draft of this manual and gave us their devoted, thoughtful, and systematic comments.

Part A: Overview

1   Introduction

"Sokorn," a Cambodian mother of ten children ages two to twenty-one, recently was referred to the project. She suffers from post-traumatic stress disorder, her husband is abusive and alcoholic, and the oldest son is a high school dropout who is now in prison.

The project director and a bilingual worker made a visit to the family to suggest to Sokorn that she and her three-year-old child join a child-parent class with two other Cambodian families in her building. The class was to take place in the apartment of one of the other families.

Despite the circumstances, Sokorn, her three-year-old, and her two-year-old fit in remarkably well. She seemed wary and held back, but she appreciated the attention shown to her children. At times she broke out of her isolation and showed some overt enthusiasm for the class activities. The children were able to join in the lessons and in the free play activities, usually assisted by other parents in the group.

Once the classes were under way we tried to assist Sokorn with her health problems so that she could better help her family. In the first few weeks of classes, she started to hemorrhage and miscarried her eleventh child. The project director arranged emergency medical treatment and numerous follow-up appointments. With the help of one of the project's bilingual counselors, Sokorn was able to communicate with a doctor for the first time. A thorough medical history was taken, and ongoing medical issues were addressed, including

mental health needs. She is now seeing a Travelers &
Immigrants Aid/Chicago Connections (TIA/CC) consulting psychiatrist to address her post-traumatic stress
symptoms.

Recently, her ten-year-old son was at home during a
child-parent class, and he admitted to the bilingual
counselor that he was not sick but stayed home from
school because he didn't know how to do his homework. The project director is recruiting a volunteer to
assist him and his siblings with school work. (Langendorf and Koch, 1995)

The purpose of this manual is to document the principles, practices, and issues of a program that has been
serving Southeast Asian and other refugees families in
Chicago during the past six years. Known as the Refugee
Families Program (RFP), it is one of the services provided
by the TIA/CC and supported by United Way of Chicago
and the State of Illinois Department of Education Even
Start program. The Erikson Institute has provided technical assistance and documentation for the project since its
inception.

During its first six years (July 1990–June 1996) the Refugee
Families Program has served 150 families: 55 percent Cambodian, 20 percent Vietnamese, 5 percent Amerasian, 3 percent Sino-Vietnamese, 6 percent Lao, 3 percent Chinese,
3 percent Afghan, and 5 percent East African (Ethiopian,
Somali, and Eritrean).

The families reside in the Uptown or Albany Park areas
of Chicago's North Side. A very large majority live below
the poverty line and are subject to the multiplicity of tensions, pressures, and life-threatening circumstances that
characterize poverty living and poverty neighborhoods.

Further, their displacement from their homelands and the
accompanying loss of familiar social and cultural supports
place both parents and children in particularly vulnerable
circumstances. All of the parents are limited English speak-
ers. Most significantly, parents have difficulty connecting
with the medical, educational, housing, welfare, occupa-

tional, and other institutions that are necessary to the well-being of their families. A paramount need, therefore, is to provide a scaffolding process that effectively connects parents and children to a range of life-supporting institutions and helps them to develop the knowledge and skill to contract and sustain those relationships on their own.

Broader Applicability of the Approaches Reported in this Manual

While the structures and processes evolved in this program were developed in the context of services to refugee families, a major premise of the manual is that these approaches can be adapted effectively to assist other populations who find themselves poorly connected to the educational and social service institutions of the society. The key problem shared by refugee and many other populations is not having the resources, understandings, skills, or accompanying self-concept that allows and encourages individuals and families to enter into effective engagement with the surrounding social/cultural world. With this problem as the focus, the program has been designed to assist families in relation to the following four goals.

1. Prepare the young children for entry into public school.

2. Enhance the parents' capacities to nurture and support the intellectual and social-emotional development of their young children.

3. Provide support to the young children's school learning after they enter public school and support the learning of the older siblings who are already enrolled in public school.

4. Promote the family's ability to be a stable and well-structured environment that (a) is effectively connected to medical and other life-supporting resources in the city and (b) can support the fulfillment of goals 1, 2, and 3 above.

Four interrelated service components are designed to meet the goals:

1. *Child-Parent Preschool Classes* (goals 1 and 2): Young children, ages three to five, and a primary caregiver (usually the mother) are joined in groups of four or five child-parent pairs. Each group normally meets in the home of one of the participating families, is culturally homogeneous, and frequently consists of close neighbors or relatives. The group meets twice a week for an hour and a half and is led by one of the project teachers. The curriculum strikes a balance between structured lessons and interactive free play, preparing children for the variety of activities that they will encounter in the public school kindergarten. Time is given to literacy development, math, art, music, and games. A major emphasis is placed on coaching and nurturing the parent's roll in fostering the development of the child. Child and parent are involved in this type of group for at least nine months.

    In some cases, where a family is geographically isolated or cannot fit easily into a group, a modified form of the curriculum is provided for a child-parent pair in their home.

2. *After-School Homework Class* (goal 3): The after-school homework class serves the older siblings of the young children in the child-parent classes and the child graduates of the child-parent classes once they have entered public school. The group meets twice a week after school and is run by bilingual workers, the project director, teachers of child-parent classes, and volunteers. The focus is on providing a context for children doing their homework, providing assistance with homework, and establishing a routine of doing homework on a daily basis.

3. *Family Service Component* (goal 4): Working one-to-one with families, the project director and bilingual staff assist families by connecting them to medical and other social service resources in the city and by assisting them in problem solving around pressing internal and external issues facing the family.

4. *Language Instruction for Parents* (goals 1–4): Project staff and volunteers provide English instruction to parents on an individual or group basis.

During years 4–6 of the program, the staff has consisted of the director (Trudi Langendorf), two teachers, two bilingual counselors, and a small number of volunteers.

The Refugees and Their Needs

The Cambodians

The Cambodians represent the largest group served by the program (55%). These families have been in the United States from four to fourteen years. The majority are from a rural agricultural background. Most of the adult women and many of the men are limited to two or three years of elementary education.

The recent history of these families stems from the attempts of the Khmer Rouge regime to destroy both the traditional rural and the Western-influenced urban cultures of the Cambodian people in the mid- and late 1970s. Wishing to establish a purist marxist agrarian society throughout Cambodia, the Khmer Rouge used tactics that included the systematic destruction of those who had more than a rudimentary education or who in any way were identified as standing in the way of the new order. Between these systematic murders and the large number of people who died of starvation, between one and two million Cambodians perished during the four years of Khmer Rouge domination.

Prior to their arrival in the United States, the Cambodian refugees had spent up to eight years in refugee camps in Thailand. Families and individuals had either trickled across the Thai border during the Khmer Rouge years or arrived in the massive exodus during the years following the Vietnamese displacement of the Khmer Rouge regime in 1979.

Among the Cambodian refugees in American cities today, a configuration of forces contributes in many cases to family tensions in both husband-wife and parent-child relationships. As with many other refugee and immigrant groups, Cambodian refugee parents have experienced widespread fatigue and depression resulting from relentless economic pressures and cultural alienation. Their abilities to deal with basic survival issues and raising children have weakened. Often they lack the energy to discipline their children consistently. Some adults cope with the pressures by abusing alcohol or by gambling, both of which contribute further to family instability.

Contributing to this very significant malaise in the Cambodian community is the trauma of the Khmer Rouge years during which almost all of the parent generation suffered terribly. Virtually all experienced the destruction of family members. They are still bearing the burden of that previous life of terror, starvation, and stress.

The Vietnamese, Amerasians, and Sino-Vietnamese

The Vietnamese constitute the second largest group served by the program (20%). Vietnamese emigration to the United States has taken a number of forms since 1975, when Vietnamese refugees began to arrive in large numbers. The first wave, arriving soon after the fall of Saigon in 1975, consisted primarily of the families of military personnel and others who were close to the South Vietnamese or American administrations in Vietnam. This group was, by and large, well educated and somewhat conversant with Western culture. Basically, they are not represented in the families now served by the program. The second wave of Vietnamese refugees consisted of the "boat people," families and individuals who managed to escape by small boat from Vietnam during the period 1979–89 and who spent considerable time in refugee camps located in Thailand, Malaysia, Indonesia, Hong Kong, and the Philippines. The boat people represent a broad spectrum of the population in Vietnam. However, they tend to be more urban than rural and considerably well educated—five to seven years of education for women and seven to nine years for men. In many cases these were families who had managed to store enough gold to purchase a boat or to purchase passage on a boat. Many of their attempts to escape were aborted through detection by the Vietnamese authorities, requiring considerable persistence to succeed.

The "Amerasians," the third wave, are families who came to the United States during the 1980s as part of a special agreement negotiated between the U.S. and Vietnamese governments. Hence, their migration period overlapped considerably with that of the boat people. A family qualified for emigration through the Amerasian program if one or more of the children in the family were fathered by an American serviceman during the Vietnamese war. A typical emigrating family consists of a mother, one or two Amerasian children, a number of other children born subsequent to 1975, and sometimes the father of the additional children. The mothers and Amerasian children in these families tend to have very limited education, resembling more the educational pattern of the Cambodians described above.

A fourth wave of Vietnamese immigration also began in the early '80s and runs to the present. Under this program, also negotiated by the U.S. and Vietnamese governments, Vietnamese refugees in the United States could arrange for the immigration of spouses, children, and parents still living in Vietnam.

The fifth and final wave of Vietnamese immigrants, starting in 1990 and continuing to the present, is the "political prisoners." Through an arrangement between the U.S. and Vietnamese governments, individuals who had been released from Vietnamese "reeducation" camps during the 1980s were allowed to immigrate with their families to the United States. These are often previous military or government personnel. Several of these families are being served by the program. Many of these individuals were severely traumatized by long exposure to abusive treatment by their captors.

The "Sino-Vietnamese" are Chinese families who had been living in Vietnam, usually since 1948. Their history of emigration from Vietnam and their educational backgrounds are, by and large, the same as those of the Vietnamese boat people described above.

At the project's inception in 1990, a considerable proportion of Vietnamese and Sino-Vietnamese families being served by the project were in the boat people category. Currently, the families being served are those who have been brought over through the Amerasian and political prisoner programs or by relatives already settled in the United States.

Basic Principles and Parameters

A number of principles operate in staff's interactions with families. These principles pervade the ideas and examples discussed throughout the manual. They include:

- Keeping a practical focus
- Maintaining a gentle, nonpushy, but persistent approach
- Keeping in mind a family's fears, sensitivities, and limitations
- Building on strengths and empowering parents at every opportunity
- Being flexible
- Maintaining confidentiality
- Maintaining boundaries of the staff role
- Maintaining staff reputation in the community

These guiding principles provide a framework for informing and maintaining staff sensitivity to a variety of cultural and individual differences between the staff and the families they serve.

Intercultural Issues

The RFP has gone through two major phases in its approach to intercultural issues. In the first phase, 1990–93, the project was staffed by three Euro-Americans: the project director and two teachers. Two major aspects of intercultural communication had to be addressed.

First was the language problem. Since the refugee parents spoke very little English, communication had to be done often through a very simplified English (somewhat resembling the abbreviated forms of pidgin English dialects) with all its inherent limitations. Translators were available occasionally, but not often enough to meet the need for consistently effective communication. This problem was least severe in the preschool classes, where the format was simple, many of the manipulative activities did not depend on language, and the overall intent was to teach English to children and parents alike.

Second, there were differences in values and norms of social behavior between parents and staff. This defined a need to educate project staff about many of the basic rules of respect that are important in Southeast Asian life: for example, taking shoes off when entering a home, abiding by a conservative dress code, not touching children's heads, refraining from personal touching among adults (especially between female staff and male members of families), and understanding that the parental inclination not to look staff straight in the eye is a mark of respect rather than a sign of reticence or avoidance.

In the second phase, 1993–96, bilingual workers, representing Cambodian, Vietnamese, and Chinese cultures, joined the project. Their addition created major breakthroughs in the family service component in which subtleties of communication were sometimes missed or had to be mediated by periodic assistance from translators working in other programs or institutions. The combination of the director's and teachers' experience and the cultural and linguistic expertise of the bilingual staff produced a major improvement in the overall effectiveness of the family service component and in the program as a whole. Among other things, the addition of the bilingual workers made it possible for the program to take on some multiproblem families that had previously presented too difficult a challenge.

Regardless of the staffing composition, a number of discrepancies between the views of staff and those of clients are inherent in the project's structure and require ongoing negotiation. These include the following:

Overall view of the relationship between project and families: From the RFP's standpoint, service to families is time-limited (governed by the limitations of funding and the need to include additional families over time), while the families tend to see services as not time-limited. Correspondingly, the aim of the RFP is to foster families' independent functioning, while the families tend to view the relationship as one of long-term companionship and involvement modeled on the extended family kinship relationships that constituted their main support structures in the traditional culture.

From the project's standpoint the services also are role-limited (confined to the defined functions of the program and rendered to those families who are explicitly enrolled in the program), while families often wish to extend services to every possible aspect of their lives.

Meanings associated with education and learning: The project image of appropriate learning for children is governed by a constructivist approach in which children are to be actively engaged with the learning environment. The adult's role is to be a stimulator and scaffolder of the learning process as well as a provider of praise and encouragement. This is very foreign to most of the parents. From the parents' perspective on education, the learning process should be based on memorization and strict adherence to the teacher's modeling of skills. In this view, learning involves fixed, concrete, highly specific content in contrast to an emphasis on the learning of widely applicable concepts. Further, explicit use of praise is viewed by many of the parents as likely to undermine the child's will to persist at learning tasks and hence as inappropriate.

The RFP staff designed the child-parent preschool classes with the idea of mediating between the parents' traditional educational beliefs, the staff's constructivist orientations, and the staff's expectations regarding the public school classrooms the children would soon be entering. Consequently, the preschool classes are structured in a more didactic way than is typical of most American preschools, while still allowing for a period of free play at the beginning of the morning (see chapter 3). Initially, many parents feel uncomfortable with the free play activities such as Play-dough or puzzles because they do not see them as relevant to school learning. However, they fairly quickly get used to them and enjoy doing them with the children (and at times without the children).

The homework assignments, typically very concrete and structured in terms of right and wrong responses, come the closest to most of the parents' ideas of appropriate education.

Parental role as facilitator of learning: Another area of discrepancy is between the RFP's aim to have parents function as learning facilitators to their preschool children in the child-parent classes and the parents' reticence to do so. The parental reticence is based partly on a strict conceptual division between teacher's and parent's roles. Teaching children school-related concepts is not seen as part of the parental role. A typical posture in Cambodian culture, for example, is to turn the child over to the school and say to the teachers, "Do what you will so that he will learn." Reticence may also stem from parents' lack of confidence in their own educational backgrounds.

From the inception of the classes, the teacher (and project director or bilingual worker when they participate in classes) continually model with the children the kind of facilitative behavior they want the parent to assume with her/his child. At an appropriate time, they communicate to the parents that they hope the parents will learn these facilitative behaviors and practice them with their children at home.

Orientations toward diet: The RFP's agenda is for parents to give their children a balanced diet by current American standards. The traditional Cambodian diet amply provides for those needs. However, in their current context, parents often give their children sugar-laden foods in amounts that staff feel are excessive. Parents often explain this as resulting from their desire to give their children the sweets they themselves did not get as children and that their children were denied in Cambodia and in the camps.

Different perspectives on medical care: Staff's goal is for parents to take on the values and perspectives of Western medicine as practiced by high-quality practitioners, especially for the diagnosis and treatment of serious health problems. The RFP takes the position that the medical services offered by the clinics and hospitals that staff recommends are in most cases better for families than traditional medicine (including home remedies) and better than most of the neighborhood practitioners of Western medicine. Hence, there is often a tension (described in chapter 7) involved in moving families toward a Western medical outlook and getting them accustomed to using medical facilities that staff deems appropriate. There is also often a discrepancy between staff's emphasis on a long-term preventive medical orientation (involving regular checkups and shots) and the more crisis-based approach to which the families are accustomed.

Psychological counseling: On occasion, staff arrives at a point when they wish to recommend psychological counseling to a family, for example, around issues of marital stress or alcoholic addiction. They often find great resistance to such suggestions. Parents tend to view people in two categories: normal and "crazy." To them, getting psychological counseling means that they are in the latter category. In cases of less severe counseling needs, staff sometimes gets around these resistances by offering counseling themself during informal conversations, for example, while driving a parent to a hospital appointment or sitting together in the clinic waiting room.

Organization of the Manual

Chapter 2, on recruitment, extends the broad overview of the program begun in the present chapter. Chapters 3–8 then describe the four program components: child-parent preschool classes (chapters 3–4), after-school homework class (chapter 5), family service component (chapters 6–7), and language instruction for parents (chapter 8). Chapters 9–11 deal with how the program is administered and coordinated. Chapter 12 reviews many of the lessons learned in the evolution of the program and provides a planning outline for those who wish to plan a related service process tailored to the needs of the populations they serve.

2 Recruitment and Follow-Up

The primary goal of recruitment is to enroll families who are in need of help in preparing their preschool children for entry into school and in supporting them through their school careers.

Other services are offered to family members in the Refugee Families Program (RFP), but each family must have a preschool-age child to be eligible.

Locating Families

Locating families to take part in the RFP is accomplished in several ways:

- Contacts with social agencies
- Contacts with community leaders
- Previous relationships with refugee families
- Social networks of participating families

In the start-up year of the RFP (1990–91), Trudi, the program director, took advantage of her existing relationships in the refugee communities to spread the word about the program and to begin the process of recruitment. Trudi had worked for ten years with the resettlement of Southeast Asian refugees. As a result she had numerous contacts in the refugee community and knew the representatives of the TIA/CC programs that served families in Albany Park and Uptown, the targeted neighborhoods. She also contacted other agencies serving refugees, including the Cambodian, Vietnamese, Laotian, and Ethiopian Mutual

Assistance Associations. Trudi met with the representatives of all these agencies and explained the RFP in detail in order to get appropriate referrals from them.

In addition to reaching agencies and organizations, Trudi talked to informal leaders and people who were pivotal to the life of the communities. The owner of the local grocery store where many families bought food, the janitor in a building housing refugee families, and others who were close to the community were good sources for finding families with young children. Gaining the trust and cooperation of community members was essential to finding the right families for the program. Eventually many of the participating families recruited other families with young children who they thought would benefit from the classes. As the program became operational it became better known in the communities, and recruitment became easier.

Initial Contacts

Once a family has been identified or refers themselves, Trudi talks with the parents and explains the RFP to them. If the parents want to join the RFP after hearing about it, they go on to the next step of enrollment.

In her initial contact with a family, Trudi often shows them photos of the preschool classes in order to give them a more tangible grasp of the program. This is particularly important when there are language or cultural barriers that might hinder a parent's understanding of the educational process used in the classes.

Although many of the families will eventually partake of the other services offered by the RFP, the most common pattern of involvement starts with enrolling parents and their preschool children in one of the child-parent classes, which normally meet in one of the participants' homes (see chapters 1 and 3).

Enrollment and Intake Interview

Each family enrolled in a child-parent class is asked if the classes can be held in their apartment. There is always at least one family who volunteers their apartment for the classes. Although some of the apartments are crowded, the teachers adjust to the situation and help the parents organize their belongings to best accommodate the class.

Some of the families with children between birth and seven years of age who are referred cannot participate in the classes for a variety of reasons, e.g., there is an ill or handicapped family member, there are too many young children in the family, the family lives too far away from the class meeting site. These families receive both educational and family services on an individual basis. A teacher or a bilingual staff member visits regularly and meets with a parent (usually the mother) and one or more of the family's young children. The home visitor introduces the parent and child (or children) to appropriate preschool activities and also provides needed services to the family. These services may include help in dealing with social agencies, such as public aid, or with a medical facility or a school. The work with the family may result in referral to another agency for services.

When explaining the details of the program to a family, Trudi describes how it will help the children get ready for school. Although there are other services provided by the RFP, Trudi keeps her initial explanation simple, focusing on the child-parent classes, which have a special appeal to the parents. An approach that emphasizes one or two aspects of a more complex program has been used by other programs that have been successful in recruiting families with preschool children. For example, in the early years of Head Start, recruiters learned that families were often most interested in enrolling their children because the program served meals. Therefore, when recruiters went into neighborhoods to inform families of the program this factor was highlighted.

Trudi always makes clear that mothers, fathers, or caregivers are expected to attend each session and to help their children with the activities. Family involvement in the preschool classes frequently leads to participation in the family service component, the after-school homework class for

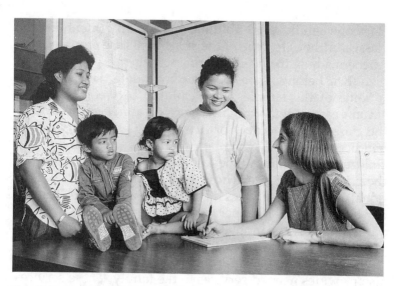

Trudi Langendorf, Program Director, describes the Refugee
Families Program to two mothers and their small children.

older children in the Albany Park area, or language instruction.

The classes are primarily for families with children
between the ages of three and five. However, mothers are
encouraged to bring their younger children since there is
often no one to care for them at home and the attendance
of parents is an integral part of the program. The younger
children gain much from the program, and the parents
begin to understand the importance of providing intellectu-
ally stimulating activities for their youngest children.

The classes are kept small, with an upper limit of five
parents and seven preschool children. Small groups make
it easier for the teacher to offer individualized attention to
the children and to keep the needs of the mothers in mind.
Since the classes meet in the apartment of one of the participants, the size of the group is also limited by the number
that can be accommodated comfortably.

Enrolling all the families in a year's program is complicated. After gathering names and addresses of possible

enrollees, finding an apartment where classes will meet, and setting a schedule, Trudi must check back with parents to ensure that they will be able to manage the proposed plan. Most of the parent contacts must be in person because language differences make it difficult to communicate on the telephone and some of the families do not have telephones.

A family's formal entry to the program begins with an intake interview administered by Trudi or a bilingual staff member (see appendix C for form used). The intake information consists of

- Names and ages of family members
- Educational background of each family member
- Work histories
- Personal histories
- Medical histories and current medical status

In cases of families who are feeling overwhelmed or who are reluctant to share their personal histories, the intake information may be gathered over a period of many contacts.

When Trudi visited Lim for the first time, she did not know that Lim had nine children and that the family had many problems. It took months of visiting and talking to Lim for the full history to come out. At first the conversation was kept on a superficial level, but as a trusting relationship developed, the full history became clear. It turned out that the children were fathered by three different men and that there were multiple health problems among the family members, including a deaf son.

At any point in the enrollment process there is the possibility that new families will hear of and want to learn more about the program.

During the first visit set up by the Vietnamese Mutual Assistance Association, Trudi was to explain the RFP to Tuyet and see if she might be interested in joining.

When Trudi arrived at Tuyet's apartment, her two neighbors were there, and all three were interested in hearing about the RFP. Trudi was able to explain the RFP to the three women, and was able to complete the intake interviews for all of them.

Follow-Up

The bilingual staff members and Trudi often visit the child-parent classes during the initial months of the program in order to build relationships with parents and to let them know about the additional services offered. Family services may include help for medical or psychological problems or support in dealing with public aid or the schools. Older children in the Albany Park area may choose to attend the after-school homework class. Adults who want to learn or improve their English can be referred to an English language class or may receive tutoring with a volunteer in their home. Frequently a teacher will identify a family she thinks might be in need of additional services. She will inform Trudi about her observations, and together they will determine if the family might be receptive to discussing the situation.

Soon after a family is engaged in the RFP, Trudi or a bilingual counselor makes a home visit as a continuation of the process of building a relationship with the family. These visits provide information that augments the intake interview. When visiting a family, the RFP staff bring toys for the children to play with, which gives the staff an opportunity to observe the children's skills and the interaction between parents and children. It may be obvious that the family is functioning reasonably well or, alternatively, seems to need additional help. The initial assessment provides a better understanding of the family, including interactions among family members and their lifestyle. It also provides a better understanding of their cultural background and how it is reflected in their views of education and their child-rearing practices. If the family is known to Trudi or the bilingual workers through earlier contacts, they have an even better understanding of the family dynamics and the family's quality of life.

Ongoing Assessment

Continuing assessment of the participant families is based on information from several sources. In addition to the early visits to the child-parent classes by Trudi and the bilingual workers and the home visits, the teacher reports provide information about the children's performance in class and the ways in which the parents interact with their children, e.g., discipline them, teach them social skills, or support their learning.

It became obvious during the early participation of Nath and his mother in the preschool class that their relationship was in serious trouble. In the class mother was harsh with Nath, scolding him constantly and even hitting him. Because the mother's discipline was so inconsistent and her intentions were so unclear, Nath never knew what she expected of him or why he was being punished. As a result, he was out of control, running around and rarely listening to his mother, and having difficulty being cooperative in the group.

A visit to Nath's home confirmed what the staff observed in the preschool class. Nath's mother seemed at a loss about how to discipline him effectively. She complained constantly about his behavior to Trudi and to other parents in the class. Her complaints were interpreted by Trudi and Nath's teacher as a plea for help.

Trudi was able to follow up with a series of talks with Nath's mother about her son's behavior. Together they planned a strategy of how she might be more consistent with him. These conversations, combined with her observations of how the teacher worked with Nath in class, helped Nath's mother change her behavior. In response to his mother's shift in her interactions with him and his experience with the teachers, Nath's behavior improved remarkably, and he was able to make a reasonably good adjustment to public school.

During the home visits, Trudi and the bilingual staff have an opportunity to talk to parents, as well as observe how family members get along. The entire staff are careful to remain sensitive to cultural differences in child-rearing practices, particularly when the practices seem to be negative at first glance. They have found it is more productive to assess how the children are getting along than to evaluate parenting techniques.

The recruitment process is an important step in the development of a family program such as the RFP. If it is designed and carried out well, it ensures that there is a good match between the goals and practices of the program and the needs of the families being served. A good match between program goals and client needs lays the groundwork for a successful program. It provides the basis for developing educational activities, family services, and referrals to appropriate clinics and agencies that benefit all members of the families.

Early and ongoing assessment helps families understand the array of services that are available to them and how they can take advantage of them. The assessment also aids the staff in understanding the needs of the families and what the RFP can do to meet those needs.

Part B: Program Components

3   Child-Parent Classes

The goals of the child-parent classes are to prepare the young children of refugee families for entry into public school and to enhance the parents' capacities to nurture and support the intellectual and emotional development of their young children.

The classes are composed of both children and parents (mostly mothers) and meet on a regular basis with the same teacher for a nine-and-a-half-month session. The objectives for the children are (1) to foster their intellectual development by concentrating on observation skills, classification skills, and basic concepts, such as more and less, large and small, etc.; (2) to develop the specific skills that will help them make good use of the elementary school curriculum, such as some basic English vocabulary like the words for colors, shapes, and commonly used phrases in the classroom ("show me," "come here," "get in line"); and (3) to learn to use the materials normally found in preschool classes like scissors, crayons, paste, puzzles, blocks, and board games. The children become familiar with the games and songs that are a part of preschool programs and with school routines. Language development is enhanced by reading to the children on a regular basis.

The acquisition of the social skills expected of children entering school is an important part of the program, and the teachers are especially careful to interweave this learning into the daily program. For example, when Joey interrupts the teacher in his eagerness to comment on the story she is reading, she gently tells him that he needs to raise his hand when he has something to say

Joanna teaches a child-parent class.

and at the same time reassures him that she is eager to hear his comments.

A Child-Parent Class

The following is a description of one class in the Refugee Family Program (RFP) and provides a picture of the activities and the interaction among the participants.

It is 9:15 on a gray November morning, and Joanna is knocking on the door of Bopha's apartment with her suitcase of toys, games, books, and snacks. She remembers to take her shoes off before entering the apartment when Bopha opens the door. Joanna begins to prepare for the class that meets here each Tuesday and Thursday from 9:30 to 11:00 AM. The class is made up of four mothers and their six children. Four of the children range in age from three to five years, and two who are not the focus of the program are two years of age.

Since this group of parents and children are Cambodian, their first language is Khmer. Only one of the mothers has a basic competency in English, but all are eager to learn.

On this day, Joanna is planning a lesson on parts of the body, using both the English and the Khmer words in the discussion. At the last session one of the mothers had asked the English word for elbow, and Joanna thought she would follow up on the question. The theme of the human body is part of the unit on "self" included in the curriculum. Plans for the session include activities that also engage the two youngest children. Joanna wants to reinforce the importance of stimulating the younger children by showing appropriate activities and games to the mothers.

Joanna puts out a variety of toys and activities, and when the group arrives each child selects something and starts to work with it. This is "free play" time, when mothers and children interact with the available materials. It is an opportunity for Joanna to observe the children and the interaction between mothers and children. After about twenty minutes, she asks everyone to put the materials away and to get ready for the "good morning" song. This activity is part of each session, and the children have learned the words and sing along with the teacher. After the song, the teacher says "hello, good morning" to each child, using his or her name, and helps the children respond in English. Next, attendance is taken, which requires each child to put a mark on the box for that day next to his or her name. The older children use the first initial of their first names instead of a check. Joanna then collects the homework that the children have brought in their folders or carryalls. Today, everyone has done his or her homework and shows it to Joanna. She puts a sticker on each child's work as she comments on it and returns it to the child. She then asks the children to return the books they borrowed at the last session, and she checks their names on her list.

After these routine activities, Joanna begins the day's lesson. She gives each child a puzzle of a person. The parents are encouraged to sit next to their children. The two-year-olds are given simple four-piece puzzles. After the children complete their puzzles, the teacher reads them a book about the parts of the body. She asks the children to repeat the parts of the body in English, and asks one of the mothers to give the appropriate Khmer words, which the children repeat.

Following the day's lesson, Joanna asks the children to help get ready for the snack, which is always nutritious and sets an example for the mothers of healthy food that their children enjoy. A couple of children give each person a napkin, a paper plate, and a paper cup. Joanna pours juice for each child and asks one of the children to pass a basket of apple slices, and another to pass a basket of crackers. The mothers are included at snack time. Today they all help themselves, although sometimes they decline. The children are almost always eager to eat, and today is no exception.

The children and the mothers help clean up after snack. Then the teacher has everyone stand in a circle and sing "Put your right hand in." Everyone follows, and the game continues using hands, feet, head, and whole self. The children enjoy the song and the movement, particularly the part that asks the children to turn about, and of course the song with movements helps reinforce the day's lesson about body parts.

Joanna then asks one of the mothers to explain that they are going to draw an outline of each of the children on a large piece of paper that the children can then color in. Each mother draws an outline of her child on the paper, with some assistance by the teacher. The children are then given crayons to color in the outline. The mothers participate along with their children, talking to them in Khmer. A few mothers guide the children's hands while they color, and the teacher gently reminds them that it doesn't matter if the result is not perfect and the children need to learn to use crayons by themselves. The teacher makes a mental note to talk to Trudi about reviewing this issue with the parents.

Joanna collects the papers, commenting about each one, and engages the children in naming or describing what they added to their outline. She prints each child's name clearly on his or her paper. Joanna then gives the new homework assignments to the parents and demonstrates what their children are to do with their help. She asks the children to choose the books they want to borrow from a selection of books she chose that morning from the RFP library. Each child selects two books. The children put their papers and books in their backpacks and get ready to leave with their mothers. Children and adults put on their shoes at the door and say goodbye to Joanna.

Curriculum and Activities

The teachers are responsible, in collaboration with the director and the consultant, for the development of the curriculum (see appendix B) and for its implementation. The curriculum provides an overall blueprint for the classes. However, teachers adapt it to meet the needs of each group, taking into account the children's ages, levels of development, and their personalities as well as the needs of the parents.

In a class of Somalian children there were four boys, ranging in age from three to six. All the boys were active and had difficulty sitting for stories and lessons. The teacher added a lot of singing, dancing, and movement to the curriculum to meet the children's need for physical activity. The result was that the boys settled down and could attend to lessons better, but because of the time spend on physical activities the teacher had to rearrange the curriculum and present new material at a slower pace.

Teachers try to take advantage of any particular interests expressed by the group and to incorporate those interests into the program. In the classroom scene described above, Joanna responded to a mother's request for the English word for elbow by including it in a lesson about body parts. The teachers also include holidays and important community events in the program.

While the class was having a snack the teacher asked the children to teach her about the Vietnamese New Year. One of the mothers helped the children recall how the holiday is celebrated. They told how they wear new dresses and go to their cousin's house for dinner. They explained they got lucky money. For the next class, the teacher had one of the mothers teach traditional songs and planned an art activity to fit the occasion. She had flowers for each of the children, which is part of the celebration, and they played Vietnamese games.

The content of the program aims at helping the children become familiar with this country's culture and the expectations of the public schools while maintaining their cultural identity. An equally important goal is supporting the children's intellectual development. The teachers are particularly careful to plan activities that foster an understanding of underlying concepts in addition to introducing the children to the familiar practices of preschool programs in this country. When Joanna brings a pumpkin to class just before Halloween, the children are curious about it and are enthralled with making it into a jack-o'-lantern. While helping the children learn about the holiday and the way it is celebrated, Joanna also makes sure to compare the triangle eyes with the upside-down triangle that is the nose. They look different, but they are really the same shape.

Preparing Materials

The teachers are responsible for bringing appropriate supplies for each session. The supplies and materials have to fit into the suitcase carried by each teacher, so they must be chosen carefully to fit the plans of the day. Teachers also select materials that provide a variety of experiences over the nine-and-a-half-month session. Toys include different kinds of blocks that offer opportunities for comparison of sizes and shapes, practice with balance, and pretend play. Art materials are included to encourage expression of ideas and feelings and provide the basis for writing. Puppets and dolls can be used to play out stories and themes about family relationships. Cars, trucks, boats, and planes support play of community activities. Books are included each day

Class Schedule

- Free play: A time when children and their parents can choose games and materials and play together or with other children and parents
- Good morning song: Sung by the whole class after they have assembled in a circle on the floor, after which the teacher greets each child by name
- Attendance: Taken with each child making a mark or his initial next to his or her name
- Homework: Collected, with the teacher offering praise and a sticker and returning the work for the child to put in his or her folder
- Teacher-led activity: A new concept or an old one reviewed related to the thematic unit being covered, for example, a felt board with felt pieces of body parts introduces new vocabulary
- Snack: Prepared and cleared with the help of the children and parents
- Art activity: Relates to the concept introduced in the teacher-led activity, with active participation by children and parents emphasized
- Reading: The teacher reads one or more books, which round out the theme of the day's lesson
- Singing, movement, and games: Used flexibly to enrich the class
- Homework assignments: Demonstrated to parents and children by the teacher and then given to each child-adult pair
- Book exchange: Children return borrowed books and choose new ones from those selected by the teacher, signing them in and out with their ''program library cards''
- Goodby song: Song by teacher, children, and parents together

to be read during class time and so that the children can borrow them to take home until the next class.

Teachers are careful to work with the family whose apartment is being used to arrange their belongings to best accommodate the class. Since it is the custom for Southeast Asians to sit on the floor, seating is easily arranged for each child and adult.

Working with Parents

The teachers' work with parents or other caregivers is accomplished in several different ways. Seating on the floor is arranged to encourage interaction between each child and his parent or caregiver. When children have trouble getting started during free play, the teacher shows parents ways of initiating play with their children. Starting to make something with the Legos and beginning a puzzle are ways to entice the children into play.

Teachers encourage parents to talk to their children while they play together by modeling techniques for them, like naming objects, describing what the child is doing, and asking questions. Some parents try out new English words; others use their native language.

Class activities are designed to include parents as much as possible. Sometimes teachers plan activities that are a step above the children's levels so that it is obvious to the parents that they are needed to help the children. Drawing outlines of the children that they can fill in and color is a good example of engaging the parents. Another example is cutting and pasting magazine pictures to make a book with a theme, such as clothing or food. Most of the children need help with these skills, and they are activities that parents enjoy.

Parents are asked to look at books with their children. Some of the parents can read them, while others can tell the story or just talk about the pictures in their own language. The program encourages the use of the family's first language at home as a way of maintaining cultural identity and allowing children to learn concepts in their first language. Although efforts are made to introduce the parents to the mores of this country, a balance is maintained by respecting the customs of their homeland. Tapes of songs in native languages are used during the classes, and parents take an active role in planning and carrying out special programs around their holidays. When the teacher hands out homework, she makes sure the parent or caregiver knows what it is about. She goes through it, describes it, demonstrates it, and reviews how it relates to the lesson of the day.

Efforts are made to include parents in all aspects of the program so that they feel that they are important to the class activities. They are encouraged to help prepare for each class and get the snack ready. Any parent who knows some English plays a major role in translating for the teacher. During the course of the school year, the parents become more active in the class activities and begin to use English more and more. Through their participation in the child-parent classes they learn what school is all about and what will be expected of their children.

The major areas of cultural differences from the teachers' point of view are (1) the parents' "doing" the work for their children; (2) their use of criticism but not praise; (3) their stress on the product rather than on the process; (4) their lack of age-appropriate expectations for their children; (5) their use of harsh discipline rather than gentler, verbal techniques.

There seem to be several reasons parents do the work for their children. First, the concept of "guiding the hand" as a way of teaching children is part of some Southeast Asian cultures and is the way many of the parents were taught. A parent actually takes a child's hand when he or she draws to teach him how to do the work correctly. Second, the parents are concerned with the product as an indicator of what the child learning. They do not see the process the child is going through as a means to an end of learning basic skills. Third, having children as young as two and a half or three attending school is unheard of in the parents' native countries, so there is a tendency to assume that the preschoolers should be doing what older children do, which often means they need a lot of help.

Omra, one of the Cambodian fathers, did everything for his son the first year the child was in school. He directed the boy to write letters during art, selected his toys during free play, and told him to copy whatever the teacher did. His son was very passive and took no initiative of his own. During the second year, when the boy was older, he began to do things on his own, and the teacher encouraged this independence by giving the father his own paper, markers, and other supplies. The teacher compromised with the father by not interfering with the letter writing at the beginning of the art activity, but made sure his son had a chance for more open-ended activities at the end of the art session.

Reluctance to praise one's children is rooted in the culture of the parents. Praising one's own children shows a lack of modesty, which is a quality that is valued in both the Cambodian and the Vietnamese cultures. Some parents do not praise children because they believe that praise makes them lazy. However, many parents who do not praise their children find it pleasurable when the teachers praise them. They also begin to see that the children respond well to praise and encouragement, and some of the parents begin to use this technique themselves.

Many parents criticize their children freely if they cannot complete a task, make a mistake, or accidentally drop or spill something. Criticism often takes the form of a parent's comparing her child with another.

One mother constantly said to her daughter, "Thanon no good," while pointing to another child and saying, "Johnny good," when she referred to their drawings.

If the parents understand any English, the teachers try to explain that there may be other reasons why a child does not perform up to expectations. The child may find the task too difficult, or may not understand what he or she is supposed to do, or may be upset about something. The teachers also explain that if a child hears that he is bad or lazy, he will start to believe it himself and will begin to act that way. The teachers also point out what the child does know or what skills the child exhibits.

The parents believe that the product alone has value, and do not count a child's scribbles as part of the process that will lead to drawing, and eventually to writing. Here too the teachers try to compromise with the parents' way of doing things. Some activities are set up to be open-ended so that the child can approach them in his or her own way, experimenting with different materials. Other projects are product-oriented so that parents can see evidence of the child's work.

The issue of discipline is a constant problem in the classes. Parents have a very different approach to disciplining and socializing their children from those used by the teachers. Many parents slap or pinch their children or yell at them. The parents were brought up this way and think it is the only way to socialize their children. The teachers model a different approach, which provides the parents with an alternative way of interacting with the children. They explain that the teachers do not hit children in school, and the children have to learn to behave without being slapped.

Cultural differences are handled mostly by compromise. The teachers try to find a middle way between the way the parents do things and the way the program functions. As relationships develop between parents and teachers, parents trust teachers to do the right thing, and the teachers see the parents' approaches in a more positive light.

Individual Services to Families

In addition to the families participating in preschool classes, some families are recruited to receive special educational services in their own homes. These families are offered special services for a variety of reasons. It may be impossible for the families to participate in the classes because of practical considerations. They may live too far from where preschool classes meet, or there may be too many young children at home for mothers to bring them all to the preschool classes. A child or adult with a handicap may be unable to travel or to be left alone. There may be a parent with psychological problems who needs more individualized attention than is possible in a group setting.

Through additional funding from Even Start, it became possible starting at the end of the third year of the RFP to provide the specialized services that these families required. With the addition of two bilingual workers to the staff, the program was able to meet the needs of these families and to provide the individualized services required by some of the non-English speaking participants.

The educational services offered in the homes of families who cannot attend the preschool classes fall into two categories. One approach follows the pattern of the preschool classes, although with some variation. The teacher visits the home of the family once a week for one and a half hours and provides activities and lessons for a preschool child and perhaps a younger sibling and either parent. Using the curriculum as a guide, the teacher plans the lessons to follow those used in the classes. Family services are provided by other staff or through referral to other agencies or specialists, and the teacher is available to parents and children on a weekly basis.

The home lessons use a more individualized approach than is possible in the classes. For example, if a child is upset because the parents have been arguing, the teacher is free to change the lesson accordingly.

> When Nancy, the bilingual worker, arrived at the Nguyen home, the mother told her she had received a letter from Vietnam that her aunt was ill. Nancy decided to talk to the mother awhile and gave the son some toys to play with. She had planned to have mother and child cut pictures from magazines and make a book, but realized that mother was too upset to participate and so changed her plan and let the little boy play by himself while she talked to mother.

There are, however, several disadvantages to home teaching. It does not provide opportunities for the children to acquire social skills in a group setting. Parents cannot observe other children, nor can they see how other parents

Jackie Holmes, a student volunteer, works with an Eritrean family.

interact with their children. They cannot share ideas or learn from each other the way parents in a group setting can.

A second approach to the educational services follows a more flexible pattern. Since home-based services have to encompass social and medical services as well as education, the once-a-week visits have to include clinic visits, appointments at public aid and other agencies, and discussions with parents about child-rearing or family problems, and it is often impossible to maintain a reliable schedule for the lessons. In these situations the educational work with the children requires a much more flexible approach and relies more heavily on play than on teacher-directed lessons. Games, drawing, and reading are provided to encourage language development and familiarity with numbers and letters.

Teacher Techniques

The following are some of the techniques that the teachers find useful in working with the children and parents who are enrolled in the program.

Modeling

Modeling is the most important technique used by teachers to demonstrate a skill or an attitude, or to show how a particular interaction results in a desired outcome. Modeling behavior for children is an effective way of communicating with them, particularly when there is a language barrier. Modeling adult-child interaction for parents has been found to be more effective than verbal explanations.

Child-rearing practices are not always transferable from one country to another. Specific techniques can be effective when they are embedded in a particular culture. When those same techniques are removed from their cultural context they may have a different meaning and may prove to be ineffective. Discipline is a good example of how cultures can clash when it comes to child rearing. Physical punishment, for example, is often the technique that the parents in the Refugee Families Program use to discipline their children, but it can be frowned upon in this country, particularly if the punishment is harsh and is seen as abuse. The teachers model a different approach to discipline, which provides the parents with an alternative method of socializing their children. The teachers explain that the children are not physically punished in school and that they have to learn to behave without being slapped or pinched.

The teachers model methods of discipline that have proven effective in this country and that can be adopted by the parents.

Lisa, one of the teachers, explains to the mothers in her class that it is important to be consistent with the children, while at the same time she is demonstrating what she does with Andy, who is very active and needs to be reminded often not to grab other children's things. The mothers, including Andy's mother, see that Andy's behavior is improving (although slowly) as the teacher consistently and kindly helps him obey the rules. Lisa also keeps in close touch with

Trudi and the bilingual staff member so they can follow up with individual help to Andy's mother as she struggles to learn new ways to guide Andy.

Teacher Interactions with Family Service Staff

The teachers are careful to note any problems they observe as parents interact with their children in the classes and to discuss these problems with Trudi and the bilingual staff. Following up on the situation described above where Lisa pointed out to the parents the importance of being consistent with children, Trudi discussed this topic with the same small group of parents. She started the discussion with an example of a mother who faced problems being consistent with several active children. The mothers in the group immediately offered a variety of solutions, ranging from spanking to ignoring. Trudi helped the mothers look at the pros and cons of each solution along with some alternatives that she suggested, including being consistent.

The goal of helping parents support and guide the development of their children is accomplished through the individual work with the parents, Trudi's occasional meetings with small groups of parents, and the child-parent classes. In the classes, mothers can see how different children behave and how the teacher interacts with each of them. The teachers provide the parents with new ways of interacting with their children and in some instances help them see their children in a different light.

An Eritrean mother has a difficult and sometimes hostile relationship with her four-and-a-half-year-old daughter. A battle of wills between mother and child has resulted in a charged pattern of disobedience on the part of the child and an increase in the mother's anger. The teacher takes several steps to help mother and daughter overcome what until now appears to be an impasse. By relating to the daughter in new ways, the teacher models for the mother alternative ways of interacting with her. Some of these new techniques include providing the daughter with choices and allowing her more time to conform to adult requests. Little by little both mother and child change, and the cycle of hostility between the two is slowly reversed and eventually changed to one of accord.

In another situation, a parent explains about the changed relationship she has with her daughter.

Choeum used to be scared of me but now I tell her what is in my heart and it helps her. Her father yells at her sometimes, but I tell him, "Her teacher talks sweet with the children; she doesn't yell. It's better."

The bilingual staff and Trudi reinforce the example set by the teachers as they discuss the reasons for the teachers' behavior and explain why it helps the children.

Meeting Individual Needs of Children

Meeting individual needs means accommodating teacher requirements to the development stage of each child, to the child's unique personality and temperament, and to his or her strengths and interests.

After a class which focused on drawing circles and squares, the children were encouraged to draw freely. Choeum and Samel made portraits. At the end of the class, we looked at each drawing. Cynthia made circles, and I praised her work. Her mother commented that I always said she did everything good, even if she didn't. I said to draw circles at her age (just three) is quite an accomplishment.

Teachers must take into account short attention spans, shyness, and difficulty communicating in English of many of the children while still making reasonable demands for participation in the class. Guiding the development and learning of each child means timing demands for "school behavior" in accordance with the increasing ability of the child to meet those requirements.

Choeum seemed less enthusiastic than usual in class today. She didn't seem interested in anything at first. I worked with her to put a 25 piece puzzle together. It was a little difficult for her, but she seemed to like the challenge. Once we were half done, she did the rest by herself. She participated well for the rest of the class.

Children have different growth rates and different learning patterns. Some catch onto new concepts quickly. And others have to mull things over before integrating new ideas. Some children mature in regular patterns, but many learn in spurts, with plateaus separating periods of growth. Teachers are most effective when they take into account these individual differences and adjust their teaching accordingly.

Gloria was not in the mood to sit in one place today. After the teacher-led activity, she was unable to sit still and moved around a lot. I did not try to make her sit down as she is very young to be sitting for a long time.

When parents have unrealistic expectations for their children, the teachers try to explain that young children in school are not expected to perform the way older children do. Since preschools are unknown in their native countries, parents assume they should be learning academic skills and find it difficult to understand how playing, singing, and listening to stories can be a way of learning. As the parents continue to attend the classes and see how the teachers interact with the children, many of them begin to see that their children are learning important skills and disciplines.

The teachers try to come to some agreement with the parents about what are age-appropriate expectations for preschool children. Although the teachers believe that academic learning can wait until the children are in public school, many of the parents urge their children to learn letters and numbers. And many of the children can and do learn these things from parents or older brothers and sisters. However, the teachers want the children to have enough time to learn basic skills and concepts, so they provide appropriate preschool activities in the classes and schedule enough time for the children to engage themselves in these activities. More structured tasks are offered for homework assignments so the parents can engage in ways that are more familiar to them.

Meeting the Needs of Parents

Teachers must also take into consideration the needs of the parents attending the classes. They too have needs that are often expressed in the class. Some of the parents want to talk to each other while the class is in session, which is disruptive and sets a poor example for the children. The teacher in one class, realizing the need the parents have for time to socialize without worrying about their children, suggested the parents come a few minutes early so that they would have a chance to chat before class starts. Another teacher suggested to the parents in her class that they use the snack time to socialize with one another. In that way they can participate with their children in the class activities and still have a chance to talk to their friends.

Helping parents feel a part of the group with an important function to fulfill makes them more comfortable. When Joanna has difficulty making herself understood while giving instructions to the class, she asks Kalyan's mother to repeat the instructions in Khmer. This provides a smooth way for Joanna to bring the parents into the activity and to help them understand what will be required of their children when they enter public school.

Although parents are expected to join the children in most of the activities for educational purposes, their participation seems to meet some of their own need to play. Since many of the parents faced difficult times and traumas when they were little, they had little opportunity to play and to engage in carefree activities. The classes meet some of the need on the part of the parents to relive some childhood pleasures.

An effort is made to maintain the same daily schedule throughout the early part of the nine-and-a-half-month cycle so that both the children and the parents can become familiar with what is going to happen and thereby gain a sense of ownership of the group. As participants become comfortable with the class and each other, teachers can be more flexible in planning activities. Toward the end of the cycle teachers are particularly concerned with keeping the parents from becoming bored and maintaining an interest and involvement in the class.

Supporting Learning

The teachers know that supporting children's efforts to learn concepts, skills, and new vocabulary can be addressed through a variety of activities. They use the entire class program to help the children learn.

> Everyone drew a lot with craypas today. Jon narrated an ongoing story while he was drawing. First he drew a flower, and asked, "What's in the flower?" He drew a bee and said, "A bee." Then he added, "and the bee is stinging him." Then he drew his father's car, and talked about that. Next, he drew some blue on the bottom and said he tripped and fell in the water. Then he drew blue over all of it and said water was pouring on him. He was very creative! He also had a spider eat the bee.

It is important for the teachers not only to help the children directly, but to help the parents encourage their children. Some parents tend to pressure their children or to do things for them; some parents scold their children or shame them when they make mistakes. The teacher takes time to help the parents support their children's efforts to learn in positive ways.

> During one class Lim's mother wrote the numbers 1–6 and wanted Lim to copy them. Lim looked overwhelmed, and her mother got upset that she wasn't doing it. The teacher went to them and suggested maybe Lim could start with a single number like 1, explaining that she doesn't know how to write yet and that's okay for her age. Her father worked with her

too when her mother left to go to the kitchen for a few minutes. He also wanted her to write the numbers, but was willing to start with 1 because the mother had explained to him what the teacher said.

Later in the day, after snack, the class made valentine cards. Lim's father worked with her, holding the paper and stencil for her. Once or twice he started coloring it for her, but the teacher encouraged him to let her try do it herself.

Just before going home, Lim started another valentine and did it all by herself.

Usually the teacher provides a model for this kind of supportive behavior, but at times one of the parents models effective behavior.

On one occasion, a father was in the class with his daughter when the activity was decorating cans using numbers to differentiate each one. Father and daughter worked very well together on their project, not only working cooperatively, but both having a good time. They provided an excellent example for the other parents.

Reinforcing Learning

An important method that the teachers employ is to review and reinforce class lessons as opportunities present themselves. All young children do better when concepts are illustrated in their everyday lives, but it is particularly important for the children in the Refugee Families Program because of the language barriers and differences in cultures. The RFP teachers incorporate this method into their repertoire as much as possible.

When there was pepperoni pizza for snack one day (which one of the mothers brought), the children enjoyed pointing out the big circle (the pizza) and the little circles (the pepperoni) after the teacher brought it to their attention. The teacher later read a book about shapes and then a book about big and little.

Self-Expression

Giving children permission to make their feelings known and providing ways in which they can express their feelings in acceptable ways are an important part of teaching in the United States. The teachers provide avenues through play, art, and music for the children to express themselves. Talking about how one feels, particularly adverse affects, is a sensitive area in many cultures. Therefore, it is most important that teachers be careful about encouraging children to express themselves in ways that are acceptable within their cultures. Art is often the best way for children to express feelings and ideas without offending anyone.

> Arnita lives in a home that is in constant turmoil. Her father has an alcohol problem, and the parents fight constantly. The older siblings are out of control, and daily life is disorganized and disruptive. But in her artwork, Arnita finds what she does not have at home. Her pictures are neat and orderly. In addition to her organization, her consistent use of her favorite color provides the structure she needs.

It is necessary to help the children learn to express themselves in ways that conform with both their own and the school's culture. A number of children are quite inhibited compared with the children they will meet when they enter school. They do not like to answer questions, and some are unable to make even simple choices, such as what to draw or which toy to select during free play time. Few children are overly aggressive or act out. When the teachers deal with the children in the class, they are modeling for the parents how to help the children be more outgoing and assertive without being disruptive or aggressive.

Creating a Sense of Community

The teachers try to create a sense of community within the classes that is consistent with the cultural ideals of many of the refugee families. For those families who have missed this kind of experience because of war and turmoil, it provides the support and nurturing that they have lacked.

A feeling of being part of a community is fostered in several ways. Both parents and children are asked to share in the group life by helping with snacks, passing out materials, putting toys away, and helping each other with more difficult projects.

When Nheum finishes his puzzle quickly and asks Joanna for another one, she suggests that he might work with Sang, who could use his help in learning how to do puzzles. Nheum immediately moves to Sang's side and picks out some pieces for her. He looks at Joanna and smiles, and she tells him what a good job he is doing. Sang also looks pleased at getting the attention of one of the older boys. Joanna thinks that maybe she should suggest that Nheum not do so much of the puzzle and that he let Sang work a little harder, but she decides to let well enough alone. She'll save that lesson for another day.

The goal of helping parents to be supportive of their children in public school is met in part by having mothers, fathers, or other caregivers participate in the child-parent classes. Here they have an opportunity to share directly in the children's activities and experience what the children are learning by working with the same materials and participating in the same projects. They see how the teacher interacts with the children, and learn by example some new ways of child rearing that are more compatible with their new life situations. In group meetings, but mostly through individual contacts with the parents, the bilingual workers and Trudi discuss specific situations that have concerned the parents, thereby helping them learn specific techniques to support their children as they enter and go through public school.

4   Group Development

While chapter 3 focused on how child-parent classes are organized and managed, chapter 4 begins to look at group dynamics.

Groups change over time, but all groups do not develop in the same way or at the same pace. Unlike individuals, groups do not have a common biological substratum that directs the course of their development. Rather, group change is based on a number of other factors. Two main elements are the individuals who make up the group and how they interact with each other, and the purposes or goals of the group. Other factors that influence group development include the environment in which the group functions, the reasons the participants join the group, and the influence of the group leader.

There are several factors that influence the way the groups in the Refugee Families Program (RFP) develop. The members of each class have some things in common, as they are recruited from the same cultural/ethnic background and have children between three and five years of age. They all have past experiences as refugees, and most share a history of persecution and the devastation of their communities. Some have endured the murder of family and friends. Families from some ethnic groups (e.g., Cambodians) live in close proximity to each other. Other ethnicities prefer not to live in such close proximity (e.g., Vietnamese), even though they may be friends or acquaintances. The previous relationships (both positive and negative) of the individual members influence their behavior within the group. Although the groups differ one from the other, a major factor in the development of group cohesiveness is the sharing by group members of the determination to help their children.

In some groups development progresses smoothly; in others it is rocky, with forward strides and backward slides. But within the nine-and-a-half-month cycle of the Refugee Families Program all the groups change, becoming more cohesive as the group members interact with a common objective and build up shared experiences.

The following is a description of the changes that took place in one group in the RFP over the period of a school year. The issues that arose at each stage of this group's development are specified, and a summary of issues that might apply to other, similar groups is included at the end of the chapter.

Description of the Group

Class AB consisted of Cambodian mothers and children who lived in the same apartment complex in Albany Park. This group was recruited by Trudi, the program director, who was familiar with the neighborhood from her previous work. The class met for one and a half hours twice a week for thirty-eight weeks.

There were five mother-child pairs in the original group. Four of the mothers were sisters; the fifth mother lived in the same building. When the group was formed, the five children who were officially part of the project were all four years of age. In addition, there were five other children (four younger and one older) who came with their mothers.

After about three months, the mother and her three children who were not related to the others dropped out of the group because she was planning to move as a means of escaping multiple family problems.

The class was originally held in the apartment of the oldest sister, Somaly. Somaly had a four-year-old daughter, Linda, and a two-year-old daughter, Monika, both of whom attended the class, although only the older child was officially part of the program. In addition, she had four other children.

About two-thirds of the way through the cycle, the class began to meet in Thuan's apartment. The change in location was made to accommodate Thuan, who was five months pregnant and had three children, ages two, three, and four.

One of the other sisters, Hien, was pregnant at the beginning of the cycle and delivered during the middle of the cycle. The birth of this child interfered with her participation in the class for a short time, but within a few weeks she came back bringing the baby along.

The fourth sister was Hong, who was the youngest and spoke English fairly well. Hong played the role of helper in the group. She acted as interpreter for the teacher, Joanna, translated messages for both Joanna and Trudi, and helped all the children whenever she could. Because Hong had only one child in the class and attended sessions regularly, she was able to play the role of "teacher's helper" successfully.

Phases of Group Development

Phase 1: Group Beginnings

The beginning of this group was characterized by confusion and chaos. Attendance was sporadic, and mothers and children often came late to class. The goals and structure of the class were not clear to the mothers, who saw the classes as a time when the children were occupied and they could visit with each other. They sat together instead of with their children. Their talking often disrupted the children's activities and interfered with what the teacher was trying to accomplish. It should be noted that these refugee mothers had virtually no formal schooling and were not aware of the requirements of "classroom behavior."

Several times during the first six weeks of classes, Trudi came with Joanna and talked with the mothers during the opening free-play period about the structure of the class. She reminded them of the time the class would meet and of the fact that everyone was expected to be on time and to attend regularly. The mothers were asked to sit with their children and to help them when they needed it. They were also asked not to talk to each other when the teacher was giving instructions or teaching. Trudi and Joanna emphasized the mothers' responsibility to help their children and to work with the teacher to make the class run smoothly. They explained how important the mothers were in helping to prepare their children for school. They also told the mothers that the children would be given homework at each class and that one of the parents or an older sibling should see that it was done and should offer help when necessary.

During this first phase the children were also initiated into the schedule and the program. However, the emphasis was on showing the children what would happen rather than on talking to them about it.

The issues for phase 1 were

1. *Establishing relationships:* This group was unusual because four out of five mothers were sisters. Therefore, the establishment of a relationship between the teacher and participants took center stage, rather than the relationship among the participants.
2. *Establishing communication channels:* In this group, Hong knew enough English to act as interpreter, which helped to solve the problem of communication.
3. *Establishing expectations for group functioning:* The institution of a set of ground rules for the functioning of the group was a central issue in the first phase. Perhaps because the sisters knew each other so well, they were freer to interact with each other than they would have been in a new situation.

Phase 2: Shift in Behaviors

The behavior of the mothers in the second phase showed a significant change. They were able to focus more on their children and cooperate with the teacher. They no longer used the class only as a chance to interact with each other and seemed to understand the class's purpose of helping the children and their role in that process. Most important, they began to enjoy the classes and activities.

The class itself ran more smoothly, but this did not mean that there were not times when it was hectic. Transitions were sometimes difficult, particularly when Hong was absent and communication broke down. The pivotal role she played in helping to keep things calm and organized became more obvious. However, on a couple of occasions when Hong was not present, the other mothers were more helpful and joined in more. Because the members were acclimated to the group, individuals were able to assume new roles when the need arose.

During this phase the teacher continued to guide the mothers in interacting with the children appropriately. The mothers were able to take in this information because it was given in context and was modeled by the teacher so that the mothers could see immediate results. This is an example of the "teachable moment." Although the mothers seemed to understand and accept the notion of helping children without "doing" for them, they were not always consistent in putting what they knew into practice.

As the children became familiar with the routine and the structure, they became more interested in the activities, which was demonstrated by their lively and enthusiastic response to them. Their skills increased, as did their understanding and use of English. The teacher was better able to assess their individual skills and capabilities. Two of the children emerged as the most capable and took the lead in review sessions, with the other children looking to them for answers.

Issues for phase 2 were

1. *Relationships:* The teacher and the participants were beginning to forge relationships, with the latter becoming friendly, while still respectful. The ground rules for the behavior of the mothers were reviewed periodically.
2. *Assessment of curriculum:* The curriculum was assessed to be appropriate for the children who were the focus of the class. The teacher had to make sure that the younger children were offered appropriate activities to demonstrate to their mothers the importance of responding to their needs and also to keep them from interrupting the older children.

3. *Meeting individual needs:* Changes were made in the location of the class to fit the needs of the mothers.

Phase 3: Developing Cohesiveness and Participation

During the third phase the mother and children who were not related to the others dropped out of the program. This changed the dynamics of the group. The group size was reduced by one adult and three children, two of whom were not preschool children. The group became more cohesive and manageable, partly because of the change in size and partly because the remaining mothers made a more cohesive unit. The children participated more in activities, as they sensed their mothers' increased comfort in the group. The children's use of English increased, and mothers used more English to communicate with their children. During the December holidays, the older children, who were home from school, were encouraged to attend classes. Because the size of the group increased, it met at a larger apartment. The mothers' attendance was erratic during this time, and the older children accompanied the younger ones instead. This gave them a chance to participate and learn more about what their siblings were doing in class. They helped the teacher, and the teacher encouraged them to help the younger ones at home.

After the holidays, things returned to normal. The mothers continued to participate appropriately in the classes, and the teacher noted that two of the mothers had really internalized ways of helping the children that would be carried on at home.

Issues for phase 3 were

1. *Further consolidation:* Consolidation of the group was furthered by a change in group membership, which was serendipitous. How the group would have progressed without this change is uncertain, but it was moving in this direction.
2. *Reaching family members:* During this phase the teacher planned to further the goals of the program to reach as many members of the families as possible. By interacting with older siblings during their holiday from

school, she was able to encourage them to help their younger brothers and sisters at home.

3. *Assessment:* The teacher assessed the progress of both the mothers and the children.

Phase 4: Deepening Relationships

This phase was characterized by deepening relationships between the teacher and the mothers and between the teacher and the children. This growth in relationships was illustrated by mothers' revealing more about their family life, including information about extended family members.

The children continued to do well with the preacademic work, but the teacher noted increasing variations among the children in their abilities to grasp the material. Perhaps these differences resulted from the content that was introduced during this phase that required more conceptual thinking.

The teacher talked to the mothers and the children about the ending of the classes and said she would miss them. Discussions included being sad about separations, which was made a part of the lesson on emotions. The teacher reminded everyone that the children would be going to public school, although not immediately. There was a party on the last day of class.

Issues for phase 4 were

1. *Separation:* Because the adults and the children in this class were all related, the focus was on the separation from the teacher.

2. *Future plans:* There was discussion of the future, including plans for further schooling for the children.

3. *Thoughts about public school:* Trudi talked to the mothers about the enrollment process in public school, and about how important it was for them to continue to help their children in kindergarten and in their future schooling.

Summary

This description of one class and of the issues that arose at each phase of its progress is meant to model how similar groups may develop and the issues that may arise at each phase. It is important for the teacher or group leader to be cognizant of the group as a whole and to be alert to its changing dynamics because he or she is responsible for ensuring that the group meets the goals of the individuals as well as those of the program.

Although groups share many similarities that help shape their development, their structures and purposes can vary from group to group, making an impact on their functioning. The histories of the individual members and the issues that are meaningful to them play an important role in the way the group functions. For example, in a group of refugees who have experienced traumatic separations, the end of the classes may arouse intense feelings in some or all of the members. The group leader must take such issues into careful consideration.

The development of this one group in the Refugee Families Program was best understood when seen in four stages. Other groups may progress differently. There may be a different number of developmental stages, the length of the stages may vary, and the rates of change may differ.

The early stages of almost all groups require a period of "getting to know each other." Patterns of communication are established, which may or may not remain constant throughout the life of the group. These patterns are more likely to change if there is a marked change in individual members of the group. The more outgoing group members may be more verbal in the beginning, but if others begin to feel more comfortable in the group, they may find their voices and the assurance to express themselves.

The role of the leader is critical in the initial stages of the group, and it is important to make that role clear to everyone. It must be decided who is responsible for setting the ground rules of the group and who must ensure that they are kept. Are the group members asked to take an active part in these early decisions and make sure everyone abides by the rules, or is it the responsibility of the leader? Because the education of both children and adults was the primary purpose in the RFP classes, the teacher was the designated leader of the group, and ground rules for conduct were decided in advance by the teacher and the program director.

It usually takes awhile for the group members to get to know each other (although in the case cited above most of the members were related) and the leader and for the children to feel more comfortable. After such an introductory period there is often a plateau when the routines of the group become known and things run fairly smoothly.

After group members feel more comfortable, other issues arise. There may be a struggle for leadership among the participants. Needy individuals may dominate the group with their demands. Individual adults may reveal their own or family problems in the group; often the revelation is made to the group leader privately. Depending on how an issue comes up and the purpose of the group, either the group addresses it or the leader alone takes action to deal with it.

Usually children's problems are manifested by their behavior. Noncooperative conduct and aggressive behavior are the more common ways that children display their discomfort. However, children can become withdrawn or abnormally quiet when something is bothering them. When problems surface suddenly, they often stem from a recent disturbance or traumatic event in the life of the child. Again, either the group as a whole (including the leader) or the leader alone has to deal with such problems.

As relationships deepen and are solidified, the group goals are brought into focus. These goals may change to meet new needs and to respond to the growth of both children and adults. Roles among group members may change, and leadership responsibilities may be taken over, or transferred, from the group leader to one or more of the adult members. Sometimes this transfer is done formally, with the change made explicit; most often it evolves slowly and is gradually accepted by all.

When the group prepares to dissolve, issues around separation arise. If the group members have grown close to one another and will not see each other again, strong feelings may surface. Feelings between group members and the leader may also be intense. On the other hand, some groups function in a businesslike manner, and strong feelings are not part of the picture when it comes time to terminate. Whatever the situation, it is important to allow individuals to express themselves in ways that are comfortable for them.

Children may also vary in their reactions to ending participation in a group. If their parents were part of the group, as was the case in the RFP classes, the attachment to the teacher or leader may not be so strong. When the group comprises only children and a leader, some, if not all, of the children usually feel very close to that adult. Like the adults, children should be offered opportunities to express their feelings about leaving.

Making plans for the future is a part of the ending process. This does not necessarily include specific plans for the group members, although it may include such plans. In the RFP classes, plans for the continuing education of the children were part of the ending process. For some of the parents, continuation of family services or referral to other services was discussed as the group meetings ended.

5 After-School Homework Classes

The goal of the after-school homework classes is to provide support to the young children's school learning after they enter public school and support the learning of the older siblings who are already enrolled in public school.

The initial goal of the after-school homework class, which was started at the beginning of the second year of the Refugee Families Program (RFP) was to support some of the older children of the participating families. It had become obvious that many of the siblings of the Cambodian preschoolers were having trouble keeping up with their classmates in school. When TIA/CC rented an apartment in Albany Park, the additional space made it possible for the RFP to offer after-school classes to the older children living in the neighborhood. Staff and volunteers helped elementary and high school students with homework and academic subjects, and the children also had opportunities to play games and to socialize in a protected environment.

The lack of school success among the children of refugee families, particularly Cambodians, is due to a number of factors. Language difficulties are, of course, a major cause of their poor academic performance, but there are a number of other forces that make an impact on school achievement. Because of their newcomer status or because they live in families rooted in other cultures, these children often feel "different." Feelings of being outsiders can result in low self-esteem and a lack of confidence, which make it difficult for the children to apply themselves to the challenging tasks that schools present. The result is a vicious cycle of hopelessness and failure.

For a variety of reasons, most of the refugee families in our program are unable to give their children what they need to succeed in school. Many families in the program are large and live in crowded apartments with limited material resources.

A high school freshman who attends the homework class told a volunteer that his parents want him to attend the classes for help but also because they like the fact that he is "out of their way."

Parents, and mothers in particular, are often overwhelmed with meeting the day-to-day requirements of the family members. In addition, many parents suffer from post-traumatic stress disorder, which is not always recognized or treated. This disorder can drain an individual's energy and cause a number of other symptoms that interfere with optimum performance.

Providing the structure necessary for living in crowded quarters in an urban environment is not part of the repertoire of many families raised in rural settings in very different cultures. This lack of structure takes its toll on the schoolchildren in the family, who are asked to meet school requirements on a daily basis.

The importance of formal schooling as a part of a child's growing up and as a means of successful adaptation to adult life is not very important in the belief system of some refugee families, particularly those coming from rural areas who have little schooling themselves. Meeting the challenges of everyday life can take priority over going to school and doing homework. Often older children are kept home from school to care for younger siblings. Parents are not acquainted with the notions of demanding that children do their homework on a regular basis or of helping them find a place to do it. Because many of the parents do not read and write English well, and many are illiterate in their own language, they are unable to help their older children with homework assignments.

Parents are also alarmed by the crime that surrounds them. The rural environments from which many come do not prepare them for life in a large city. Parents often feel helpless about keeping their children safe from the dangers of the streets and the many attractions offered to youngsters today in an urban setting. They look to the after-school homework class to provide supervised activities for their children.

At a parents' meeting, a Cambodian father said, "I don't have to worry about my kids being on the streets when they are in the homework class."

In addition, some of the schools do not offer the kind of support that refugee children require. Many of the teachers have no training in the special needs of limited-English children and little understanding of those who are newcomers to the city. As a result, school is not a satisfying experience, and the children are easy prey to life on the streets and the camaraderie offered by the gangs.

A freshman reported that she had to "sneak out of the house to come to class" that day because she told her parents she was too sick to go to school. Apparently homework classes are more inviting than regular school.

The after-school homework class is part of the effort to compensate for the barriers that older siblings face in negotiating the school system. These adolescents and school-age children, all of whom are Cambodian, are invited to come to the apartment rented by TIA/CC in a building in the neighborhood. The building, housing about twenty Cambodian families, is close to many of the neediest families. The apartment consists of two bedrooms, a kitchen, a large closet/pantry space in which games, paper, and art materials are stored, a bathroom, and a living room.

Although the original plan was to provide homework classes for about fifteen older siblings of the children in the preschool classes, soon these youths began bringing their friends. In addition, younger children, some of whom were graduates of the preschool classes, tagged along, and the group grew to forty or fifty, ranging in age from three to sixteen. Because all the children live close by and some in

Lisa, one of the teachers, helps a boy with homework in an after-school class.

the same building, it is difficult to deny them use of the classes. In time it became an explicit policy to try to include the graduates of the preschool classes who were able to attend. The homework classes provide an obviously needed service to the Cambodian community.

The class meets for two hours twice a week after school so the children can have a place to do their homework and to have help from teachers, bilingual staff, volunteers, and the program director, who are available at each meeting. Some children do not understand their assignments and need just a little help to follow the directions. Others need a lot more help and are provided with individual or small-group tutoring in reading, writing, or other academic skills.

The children are divided into three groups: children between the ages of three and seven years, children eight to twelve, and adolescents. The youngest children generally congregate in the first room. They sit on floor mats and have a variety of dittos, coloring sheets, or cut-and-paste activities to choose from. There are scissors, glue, markers, crayons, pencils, and paper available as well.

Five little children, between the ages of three and six, sit on mats drawing pictures on plain white paper. One little boy practices the first letter of his name over and over again. A volunteer sits down with him and shows him the next letter in his name. He does not speak, but immediately adds that letter to his page.

The children also have their own folders, stored in a bin in the pantry, in which they keep their art projects and papers. Three times a year the teachers and bilingual staff compile these papers into books that are presented to the parents at one of their meetings.

Some of the children in the eight-to-twelve group sit in desk chairs on the periphery of this room and do their homework. If one of the adults sees a child not engaged in a productive activity, he or she helps the child get started on the homework assignment or another constructive activity. Children in the same grade tend to sit together and work collectively. If they cannot understand or complete the assignment, they ask an adult for help. There are usually two or three adults available in this room. Frequently one or two mothers come to class, either to discuss a problem with Trudi or to spend some time with her children.

Two third-graders sit together doing their spelling homework. Both girls are working on the same assignment. They are to copy a list of fifteen nouns five times each and then use each in a sentence. Since the lesson is about making singular nouns into plurals, the volunteer asks them if they are supposed to use the singular or the plural of the words in the sentence. They do not know. The volunteer thinks it makes more sense to use the plural form, so that is what they do.

The second area in the back of the apartment is used by older elementary and some high school youths. They sit at tables to do their homework; some use chalkboards hung on the walls to work out math problems. One or two adults are usually in this room helping small clusters of students. Those who complete their homework have the option of playing board games such as chess or checkers.

Two fourteen-year-olds sit together with a chalkboard and a calculator, working on math problems. They are so focused on their work that they ignore the commotion around them, as kids talk and call to one another and move from room to room. It is a half hour before the two boys come up for air.

In the third area some of the adolescents, who have finished their homework or do not need help with it, meet with Mr. Chey from the Cambodian Association of Illinois to learn Khmer or to practice Cambodian dances that they perform at the New Year celebration. Usually some younger children join in this group's activities. Both adolescents and school-age children enjoy their time with Mr. Chey. It is a valuable addition to the homework class, and it strengthens the children's cultural identity and thereby boosts their self-esteem.

There is always a good deal of socializing and friendly teasing, both among the children and among the adults. The whole atmosphere is warm, friendly, and bustling. Sometimes the noise level is high and things seem a bit hectic, but there is little conflict or hostility expressed by the children, and the homework does get done for the most part. The children and adolescents are given a great deal of autonomy, and they handle it well, staying productive and busy as well as cooperative and helpful to one another.

The children derive a great deal from these classes. In addition to doing their homework and having special tutoring with their school subjects, they have a chance to socialize with their friends in a safe, friendly place. Since the neighborhoods where they live are not safe, having a friendly, secure place to meet their peers and just "hang out" makes a considerable contribution to their lives. This is particularly important for the adolescents, who need the

A group of Cambodian youngsters perform at the Daley Center the dances they learned with Mr. Chey in the after-school class.

companionship of their peers but are most at risk for being victims on the streets.

A thirteen-year-old girl said she likes to come to the classes because she can meet her friends. She also uses the time to read for recreation. Her friend, a young man who is a sophomore in high school, likes to play board games or cards. He also "helps the little kids with their homework." Both these young people emphasize that "hanging out with their friends" is an important part of homework class.

Parents are pleased that their children have a place that is supervised to read and do homework. They prefer the homework class to the library, which they feel is not supervised. Their concern about supervision arises from their strict standards about boy-girl relationships and the need for adult oversight.

The after-school classes have proven to be a vital comp

nent in the overall configuration of the Refugee Families Program. The children's continued attachment to the staff and their use of the structure and guidance offered by the after-school class point up the need for ongoing support for many of the children and families. The homework classes also demonstrate the need for different approaches to the education of newcomers to this country and of other groups that are alienated from the mainstream society.

6 Family Service, Part 1: An Overview

The goal of the family service component is to help families deal with vital areas of family functioning by (1) facilitating relationships with outside institutions such as hospitals, clinics, the Department of Public Aid, schools, law enforcement agencies, and public utilities; (2) helping families deal with internal family issues such as parent-child relationships, household management, and domestic violence.

Staff's first priority is to provide whatever assistance is necessary to deal effectively with needs in the here-and-now. The guiding principle in meeting this objective is "Do what is needed and the family does the rest." The next priority is to provide service in a manner that leads to less family dependency on the Refugee Families Program (RFP). This involves building on the family's strengths, increasing the family's knowledge and skills, and helping to develop a family's self-confidence, overall functioning, and connections with relevant service institutions in the city.

Services to families are provided by the program director, three part-time bilingual workers (hours totaling fifty per week for the three), and volunteers. In the most recent two-year period (July 1994–July 1996) the RFP supported one hundred families.

Phases in Relationships with Families

Relationships with families can be thought of as unfolding in three broad phases. Throughout all three phases the ongoing building and renewal of relationships with the family is paramount.

Phase 1: Establishing a Helping Relationship

The RFP staff works to establish a relationship in which a family will communicate their problems and be open to offers of help.

The manner in which staff approaches the initial work with families is dependent upon the history of their previous relationship with the family. For example, if the family is completely unknown, especially if they are fearful or feeling overwhelmed, a gentle and slow process of making contact is followed. Trudi and the bilingual worker often make use of the child-parent classes as a means to become familiar with the whole family. This can be less intimidating than a one-to-one interview. Staff is never rushed about getting all the pertinent information and is intent on not overwhelming a person with a barrage of questions at the outset.

When starting a relationship with a new family, it is virtually always helpful to assist with concrete, practical matters. This is especially true if the matter is relatively easily resolved, such as a confusion with Public Aid. Such assistance can help to build a family's confidence in the program and encourage them to seek out program assistance for more complicated or personal issues. (See Kaplan, 1986.)

Sometimes, at the beginning of a relationship, staff approaches problems in a roundabout manner, providing parents with an opportunity to confide a particular problem. For example:

> Having heard through the grapevine that Kuntheary was having a problem with her husband, Trudi dropped by to see Kuntheary. She opened the conversation by inquiring whether Kuntheary would like to come to the RFP office and select some children's clothing from the special clothing supply maintained by the TIA/CC. Kuntheary accepted the offer gratefully. From there the conversation turned to Kuntheary's concerns about her husband. He was gambling away his paycheck every Friday, drinking heavily, and Kuntheary

was afraid he might lose his job, which would seriously diminish their already meager financial resources. She also told Trudi about her husband beating her up and threatening the children. These episodes tended to occur after he had lost money in a drunken condition.

Over the next few months Trudi made several home visits to Kuntheary. One time she brought bags of donated clothing for the children. Another time she dropped by to check up on the overall well-being of the family. During these conversations it was clear that Kuntheary's husband's gambling and drinking were continuing. Trudi and Kuntheary spent time thinking through ways that Kuntheary might be able to make some money on her own. This would be money that she could control and use to feed her family.

Phase 2: Playing Out the Helping Relationship
This stage is reached when there is a mutual understanding between the RFP and family about the existence of a helping relationship. The family now trusts staff enough to make such a relationship possible and is taking some initiative in requesting assistance from the RFP program staff.

In the case of Kuntheary, the relationship entered this stage when Kuntheary made a practice of occasionally calling Trudi to come and see her. Their conversations regarding Kuntheary's pursuit of an independent income continued. Kuntheary began by taking a sewing piecework that she did at home on an industrial sewing machine, which many of the Cambodian mothers do to supplement their income. She also began to cook things at home to sell at the main Asian shopping street in the area. Somewhat later, she began purchasing flawed items from a local thrift store, took them home, repaired them, and resold them at slightly higher prices.

Once Kuntheary began to develop some income, Trudi told Kuntheary's husband about the substance abuse prevention program run by a Cambodian worker at TIA/CC. Darin (Kuntheary's husband) began to attend, but his participation was sporadic and yielded little significant change in his behavior.

Often in Phase 2 there is more sharing of the family's life and history in a trusting, intimate way. For example, one of the classes took place in the home of a former Vietnamese political prisoner family. In addition to conducting the child-parent classes in the family apartment, the teacher was giving the family English instruction. In time the wife began to share photos of her Vietnam childhood with the teacher. Then the family invited the teacher to lunch, included her in a child's birthday party, and taught her how to make Vietnamese dishes.

As the trust and intimacy deepens, however, it is essential for staff to find all possible ways to build on the family's strengths, maximizing the family's contribution to the solution of problems that arise.

Phase 3: Budding Autonomy

The family is still asking for help but showing signs of autonomy in meeting its needs (includes having increasing connectedness to service institutions).

In Kuntheary's case, her abilities in English and her overall sense of positive adaptation are good enough for her to be able to take a job at the school as a home visitor to Cambodian families.

Gathering Information

In the context of these unfolding relationships, staff gather information about families in a variety of ways:

1. Background information from the referral source. For example, Trudi learned from the referring mental health worker about Thien's severe anxiety resulting from his ten years of imprisonment and as a result made every effort to approach him gradually and to give him a maximum of control in each encounter.

2. Ongoing observations of children or parents. For example, Lisa noticed that the Nin children seemed cold during class and asked if they have sweaters. Trudi noticed Lach's infected eye when visiting the home. Choulie (bilingual worker) noticed that Savan is looking weary in class and inquired to find out whether she is pregnant.
3. Inquiries about each family's health as a systematic part of visits to homes.
4. Information learned through the family's social network.
5. Relaxed conversations when accompanying families to appointments.
6. Records of institutions with which the families are involved.

Identifying and Working on Problems

Most of the work with families centers on seeking solutions to problems. These problems are identified in one of three ways:

1. Problems that a family identifies and wants to resolve; for example, loss of food stamps or a wife's concern about her husband's increased gambling behavior. In the early stages of the relationship a family may be hesitant to communicate their need to staff. Cambodian families, in particular, can be reluctant to initiate discussion about their own problems, even though they may welcome intervention on their behalf.
2. Problems that RFP staff identify and bring to the attention of the family; for example, noticing a gas leak in the apartment that had not been noticed by the family members or becoming aware of a delinquent pattern of behavior in one of the older children.
3. Issues that RFP staff identify and decide to take on but do not explicitly share as a problem with the family; for example, enhancing a mother's appreciation of her children's abilities or working on a mother's self-esteem.

The staff's method of working with a family on any particular issue depends on an assessment of the factors working for and against a successful resolution. The following chart lists a number of the factors commonly encountered in the RFP.

Family Factors Working For Problem Resolution	*Family Factors Working Against Problem Resolution*
Family's ability and willingness to identify a state of affairs as problematic (something requiring solution).	Failure to recognize a state of affairs as a problem that needs attention.
	Fears about making the problem manifest.
Willingness to place a high priority on dealing with the problem.	Dealing with the problem is not a priority. Other pressures and concerns are more demanding.
	Fears about engaging in actions and procedures that will deal with the problem effectively.
Belief that a solution can in fact be achieved.	Pessimism about possibility for solution. Belief that the problem is part of life's natural afflictions and to be accepted without thought of change.
Energy and well-being to actively problem-solve.	Lack of the energy to problem-solve due to physical or mental illness.
Ability to speak English.	Inability to speak English.
Knowledge of how a particular service institution works.	Lack of understanding about the aims, processes, and procedures that are involved in an institution.
Other strengths that can be mobilized in support of taking effective action.	Lack of skills or other strengths that are needed to take action.
Sufficient material resources (such as bus fare or child care help) to support action.	Insufficient material resources to support action.
Awareness of and contact with a bilingual worker in an institution.	Feeling of isolation from the personnel in an institution.

RFP assistance is most needed when the factors *working against* the effective resolution of problems are more weighty then the factors *working for* their successful resolution. The task of RFP staff is to help alter the equation by creating greater weight on the side of factors working for an effective resolution. The staff does this either by introducing their own skills, knowledge, resources, and energies to become a partner with the family or by helping parents to increase their skills, knowledge, and motivation and reducing their fears. It is usually a combination of the two. In some cases, the weight of the negative forces is so great that staff has to refer to the helping role of another agency; for example, in a case of severe alcohol abuse.

The following example illustrates how some of these family factors come to play in a particular case.

Thao's Seizures and the Medicine Chart

When Trudi paid her first home visit to Nga, a twenty-five-year-old Amerasian woman, she noticed that Nga's daughter Thao had a droopy eye. She asked Nga about Thao's situation and discovered that she had been diagnosed as having a "seizure disorder." At twelve months, Thao was still unable to sit up unassisted. Nga told Trudi that Thao had been to see a doctor at Children's Memorial Hospital and he had placed Thao on medication. He instructed Nga that she needed to bring Thao in for follow-up visits in order to monitor the effects of different drugs on her seizures. However, since Thao continued to have some sort of seizures, Nga stopped bringing Thao to the hospital. Instead she began going to an internist in her neighborhood. This doctor did not set regular appointments for monitoring Thao's medication. When the prescription ran out, Nga did not know that she should request refills. Soon the frequency and severity of Thao's seizures increased.

Trudi saw the situation as serious. Thao obviously was not being well cared for by the local doctor. Trudi examined Nga's "blue card," issued by Children's Memorial Hospital, on which relevant information, including the doctor's name, is listed. She made an appointment with this doctor and the following week took Nga and Thao to the appointment. Trudi continued to set up follow-up appointments and accompany Nga and Thao until Nancy, a Vietnamese-speaking bilingual worker, began working with the family.

Nancy now handles most of the hospital visits with Nga and Thao, driving them there, confirming appointments, and explaining procedures to Nga. Nancy and the doctor helped Nga start keeping a chart tracking Thao's condition with information about length and time of day of her seizures and what medications she is taking. This not only helps the doctor find the most appropriate medications to control Thao's seizures, but also increases Nga's sense of agency in relation to this problem. Although the medical condition is not fully within her control, Nga's ability to organize relevant information that can help her daughter is important for alleviating the sense of powerlessness Thao's situation may have created.

Thao's seizures have become significantly less frequent, but she is still required to go in for doctor visits every few months.

Nga is now able to call the office to inform Trudi or Nancy about current health problems with Thao, such as negative reactions to new medicines, fevers, and the like.

In retrospect, Trudi concluded that on Nga's initial visit to the hospital with Thao there had been poor communication between the doctor and Nga concerning what to expect while Thao was on the medication. Nga did not understand that while taking the medicine Thao might continue to have some seizures, but that the seizures would be shorter, less frequent, and, hence, less damaging. As a result, when the seizures persisted, even in a milder form, Nga did not have a sense that the medication was helping.

In this episode the problem becomes identified as a result of the staff member's observation of Thao's droopy eye. Nga, the mother, had apparently become resigned to Thao's seizures as something beyond solution or amelioration. Through the staff member's inquiries, insistence, and scaffolding of the family's relationship with the hospital, a new equilibrium was established—one in which the infant's well-being was significantly improved and the mother was empowered to help her child.

The Nga and Thao episode relates to a set of questions that can help organize our understanding of the family service component:

1. *How did the need become manifest?* In this case the staff member observed the child's droopy eye on the first visit and made inquiries.
2. *How was the need crystallized into a problem to be addressed, and who made the decision?* The program director convinced the parent that the need had to be addressed.
3. *What was the staff's assessment of the forces for and against effective action?* Positive forces were (a) Nga's readiness to place a priority on dealing with seizures, temporarily eclipsed by her pessimism concerning possible remedies; (b) Nga's ability to keep records on her child's seizure patterns and hence take a collaborative role with the doctor; (c) Nga's conscientiousness in regard to giving medicine and taking care of her child; and (d) Nga's trust in the staff, strong enough to motivate her to stay in communication with them about Thao's condition.

   Negative forces were: (a) Nga's pessimism about the possibility of a solution; (b) Nga's tendency toward psychic denial of the severity of Thao's condition; (c) other family problems, including a difficult mother and an abusive husband, that were diverting her energies and wearing her down; (d) Nga's inability to speak English; (e) lack of knowledge of the institution and how to establish full communication with medical personnel.

4. *What action was implemented? Was it consistent with the assessment? Was it consistent with the principle of "Do what is needed and let the family do the rest?"* In this case, Trudi decided to scaffold the situation by making inquiries into the history of the case, making appointments, accompanying Nga and Thao to appointments, and helping to strengthen the communication between Nga and the doctor.

5. *Does the action achieve some resolution of the problem? Does it maximize the family's movement toward greater autonomy in dealing with this or similar problems?* In this case, Nga took Thao to a special child development center at Illinois Masonic Hospital for a comprehensive evaluation. This in turn led Nga to enroll Thao and herself in physical therapy sessions. Nga also agreed to have Thao enrolled as a special needs child in the Chicago Board of Education, rather than wait until kindergarten to deal with the issue of schooling for Thao.

Bureaucratic Navigating

Bureaucratic navigating refers to the staff's role in helping families to achieve effective connections with the institutions with which they need to interact to assure their well-being; e.g., clinics, hospitals, Department of Housing, Department of Public Aid, police department, public utilities, and the schools.

Barriers that stand in the way of effective relationships include the family's inability to read, speak, or write English, lack of understanding of which institution can best serve a need, lack of understanding of the roles and procedures within these institutions, an ill-defined understanding of what a proper response on the part of the institution should be, deeply rooted fears of the unknown or unfamiliar, and a distrust of bureaucracies in particular. Barriers also include a lack of time and energy, lack of understanding of public transportation, insufficient resources to pay for transportation or child care, and sometimes a state of personal disorganization that precludes taking effective action even if many of the other barriers are not present.

Another set of barriers sometimes lies in an institution's nonresponsiveness. For example, a family may receive more conscientious medical treatment when a RFP staff member is at the appointment than when there is no staff present.

The case of Thao's seizures, cited above, is a major example of bureaucratic navigating. The following are brief descriptions of other episodes that illustrate staff's bureaucratic navigating role:

Bing has problems understanding a letter from the Chicago Housing Authority. Trudi makes several phone calls to the agency and explains the content to Bing.

Savan has been told by a doctor that her child should be taken to a specialist because of chronic vomiting. The doctor makes a referral, but Savan never follows up because she does not know how to take the next steps. Trudi locates the specialist, makes the appointment, and accompanies Savan and her child to the clinic.

Public Aid undergoes a massive shift in policy that requires most of the families to go to different clinics and hospitals than they had frequented in the past. The announcements were sent out by letter in English and Spanish only. All the written notification in the world would not have effectively communicated to the families without RFP assistance.

The RFP gets Kheng's food stamps reinstated after they were discontinued through a major misunderstanding. Untangling Public Aid requires a substantial amount of time tracking down people by phone as well as trying to find out what paper trail to follow and where— then figuring out how to rectify the situation before the family goes hungry. Trudi often calls from the family's apartment in order to model ways of relating to institutions.

Nancy (bilingual worker) facilitates the communication between Nhien and the staff at her deaf son Tien's school. The social worker at the school requested that Nhien help Tien with his sign language at home and that she enforce more consistent discipline. Nancy accompanies Nhien to sign language classes at the school, where she assists Nhien by translating from English into Vietnamese during the classes.

Staff is making sure that the younger children of the Nin family get enrolled in preschool and kindergarten at the appropriate times.

Trudi accompanies Chhuon and his mother, Chhoeur, to his court appearance where Chhuon is sentenced to one year in prison for drug handling and possession of a loaded gun. She explains the process and outcomes as they occur. Trudi continues to act as a go-between for Chhuon and his mother and Chhuon's public defender as well as his probation officer.

Relating to Issues within Families

Staff's most frequent intervention in the internal dynamics of family life is in the area of parent-child relationships. The following are some examples.

Nancy (bilingual worker) wants Nhien to see her young children as smart. She brings electronic games to the home and teaches the children how to use them.

RFP staff acts as an advocate for the children of an alcoholic family. "The children are gradually being trained to take care of themselves," the older children taking care of the younger. Lisa picks up books from the office and brings them to the home. Staff is trying to show the mother the importance of observing and acknowledging her children's accomplishments. Lisa picks up the children on her way to the homework class, ensuring that they come regularly. Choulie and Trudi enroll the younger children in a state prekindergarten program.

Nancy is working on Nhien's communications with her deaf son and is trying to get her to think about the quality of her relationships with her children. She talks to her about the importance of explaining things to them rather than being physically punitive.

Kuntheary is concerned about Mony's academic work. Trudi encourages her to back off and make learning more fun for Mony.

Trudi helps Saman understand the implication of her teenage daughter's becoming deeply involved with a local gang. She helps Saman and her family make the necessary arrangements to move the family quickly to a safer location.

Work on internal issues may involve helping a family to bring more order to their daily existence. For example, Trudi helps Nhien sort all her papers and make a filing system for them.

Most poignantly, internal issues often concern domestic violence, addictive gambling, or substance abuse. Sometimes staff can work around such issues, as in the case of Kuntheary above. In most cases, however, staff refers the family to a specialized program within TIA/CC or to another agency.

Pervasive Principles

A number of the basic principles that were set out in chapter 1 regarding staff's interactions with families are evident in the approaches and scenarios presented in this chapter. They include (1) keeping a practical focus; (2) maintaining a gentle, nonpushy, but persistent approach; (3) keeping in mind a family's fears, sensitivities, and limitations; (4) building on strengths, and (5) being flexible.

Some of the other principles listed in chapter 1 need further comment in the context of the family service component.

1. *Maintaining confidentiality:* The strength of a relation-ship with any family rests on the confidence of the family that the staff has their total well-being in mind. Any breach of confidence about family matters could result in a family's feeling betrayed and vulnerable. Staff always needs to be vigilant in making sure that they adhere to this principle.

2. *Maintaining boundaries of the staff role:* Sometimes staff are requested by families and/or tempted by their own goodwill to help in ways that are either outside of their area of expertise or outside of their role definition. The program policy is to find alternatives to taking on such functions themselves.

Kuntheary asked Trudi to become involved in dealing with a real estate company that had put Kuntheary's family in a compromising position. Trudi referred the family to a real estate lawyer, rather than give advice or intervene directly in the matter.

3. *Maintaining staff reputation in the community:* Staff's overall effectiveness in the community is dependent upon their general moral standing in the eyes of the very large majority of community members. It is there-fore necessary that they always conduct themselves in a manner that respects community norms. This is another area in which knowledge of the culture plays a vital role. Staff also needs to avoid unnecessary asso-ciations with individuals of questionable moral repute in the eyes of the community.

To help a teenage boy who was in trouble with the law, it was suggested to Trudi that she seek some vitally needed information from someone who had an unsavory reputation in the Cambodian community. She decided to forgo this suggestion in order to main-tain her reputation as someone who associates with appropriate individuals.

7 Family Service, Part 2: Helping Families to Be Healthy

The overall medical goal of the Refugee Families Program (RFP) is to help families achieve and maintain the health of their members. In the context of this goal, the RFP has two major objectives: to facilitate use of adequate medical care and promote each family's autonomy in seeking and responding to medical care. The pursuit of each of these objectives is complex.

Health Issues among the Participating Families

Ninety-five percent of the families served by the RFP experience serious medical issues that require professional health assistance. A partial list of these medical problems includes asthma, allergies, blindness, deafness, paralysis, migraines, gynecological disorders, post-traumatic stress disorder, ulcers, pre- and postnatal complications, as well as the normal gamut of childhood illnesses, and emergencies like cuts and gunshot wounds. Most of the families are poorly connected to adequate medical resources. As a result, 65 percent of all the family service work in the RFP is focused on health-related matters.

In many cases the medical need is so serious that failure to resolve it prolongs the malfunctioning of the family and precludes other effective work with the family. An example of this is the case of Vechra, who had not seen a doctor for years and had several untreated health problems. Her blinding migraine headaches now caused her so much pain and left her so exhausted that she could barely participate with her child in the program's preschool classes, nor did she have the energy to work with her children on school-related projects at home. However, once her migraines subsided as a result of taking the appropriate medicine, her involvement with her children and their schoolwork increased significantly.

Specific Medical Needs and Related Risk Factors

Physical ailments and problems related to getting appropriate medical care are exacerbated in this community for many reasons. Basic poverty, lack of decent housing (i.e., pest-free, clean, uncrowded), past histories of poor medical care, poor understanding of Western medicine, and some parents' inability to provide adequately nutritious food and weather-appropriate clothing are some of the reasons why so many of the RFP families need extensive medical attention. In most families there is also a lack of preventive care and infrequent early detection and response to symptoms.

Family composition and dynamics are another major contributor to health problems. The mothers usually are the primary family caretakers, often with little or no support from their husbands, and sometimes in spite of their husbands, some of whom are actively destructive or abusive. A woman trying to tend to several small children (often five or more), in a cramped (usually one-bedroom) apartment, with very limited resources (money, time, energy, outside help), is barely managing to keep up. The family's overwhelming stress often results in a crisis-by-crisis orientation to life. Frequently there is no awareness of preventive care or notion of "nipping a problem in the bud." It is difficult for a person inundated by multiple stresses to see beyond the immediate situation and take action to keep a full-blown crisis from developing. For example, a child with a minor toothache will not be taken to the dentist until it has become painfully infected and RFP staff is called in for help. Similarly, a parent who has managed to get a child to see a doctor may not be diligent about getting that child to follow-up appointments because the problem appears to have been alleviated, even if monitoring of medicines is required.

Considerations in Responding to a Family's Medical Needs

A range of considerations come to bear in dealing with a family's medical issues. These include the RFP staff's perception of the medical problem that is presented, the family's perception of the symptoms and their meaning, available medical resources, staff's current relationship with the family, and the characteristics of the family, including the parents' educational level and the family's established patterns of dealing with health problems. The case of Vechra gives us an example of how some of these factors affect the program's ways of working with a family on their medical issues.

Vechra, the Angry Doctor, and the Big Machine

When Vechra had a new baby in October, the bilingual worker Choulie asked Vechra how she was feeling. After repeated questioning, Vechra told Choulie of partial paralysis she had been experiencing on one side of her body since becoming pregnant with that child. She also had been experiencing severe headaches.

Choulie obtained more details concerning the nature of Vechra's problem: what her symptoms were, if she was seeking some kind of health care, and if that had provided any relief. It turned out that Vechra was seeing neighborhood doctors and taking traditional medicines but nothing was helping. Trudi offered to take Vechra to the general medicine clinic at Hospital A with Choulie. After making the appointment she drove Vechra and Choulie to the hospital in early December. She dropped them off and Choulie accompanied Vechra on her first visit.

Vechra was given blood tests, and the doctor prescribed migraine medicine and scheduled an MRI (magnetic resonance imaging, a brain scan). Trudi picked up Vechra and Choulie after this appointment, and later Choulie told Trudi about the visit. Vechra had been extremely nervous because she had rarely been to a Western doctor and was unaccustomed to the physical exam, especially one practiced by a male physician. She was asked to undress and given a full neurological exam, which involves the doctor touching the patient from head to toe. On top of all these uncomfortable aspects of the visit, the doctor lacked interpersonal skills and had a harsh manner, which contributed to Vechra's anxiety. At one point during the exam the doctor asked Vechra to describe his touch as feeling weaker or stronger on either side of her body. Trudi had previously explained to Choulie that her translation of Vechra's answers must be as literal as possible because paraphrasing could result in miscommunication between the doctor and patient. Consequently, Choulie told the doctor that Vechra said, "One side itches and one side tickles." All the while, Vechra was giggling as a result of her extreme discomfort with the whole situation—a typical reaction of a Cambodian woman to an awkward situation. At this point the doctor blew up at them, shouting that he had said "stronger or weaker," not "tickles or itches," that he had a waiting room full of people, that Vechra was not taking the exam seriously and they were wasting his time. The doctor had no understanding of the fact that Vechra was not used to this kind of exam and that she was embarrassed and frightened. He was also unaware that her giggling was an expression of discomfort and not necessarily a sign of someone who is not taking the situation seriously.

An appointment was made for Vechra to get an MRI on 20 December. Trudi asked the doctor, who had explained nothing of the procedure to his patient, for a sedative to calm the anxious Vechra. Trudi explained the procedure to her as they drove home in the car, trying to give her some sense of what to expect, the loud noise she would hear and the tight tunnel she would be placed in. After Vechra's experience with this angry and uncommunicative doctor, in Trudi's estimation she would not have followed through with the MRI or other treatment had it not been for the time RFP staff took to reassure her. On the day of the MRI Trudi once again picked up Choulie and Vechra at the hospital. She asked them how it went, and if it was scary for Vechra. Vechra replied that because it had been explained to her, it was not so frightening.

Because the doctor had acted so disrespectfully to both Vechra and Choulie, Trudi decided to accompany them to the next appointment in order to observe the interpersonal dynamics and to intervene if and when appropriate. On their next appointment on 23 December, Trudi sat in on the exam. She sat slightly behind and to the side of the doctor in order that he would talk directly to Vechra through Choulie, who were both sitting straight across from him. Despite all of this the doctor swiveled in his chair to talk to Trudi—yet another sign of his disrespect and discomfort. Although his manners had not improved much, Choulie said that his demeanor was completely different with Trudi present—not charming but also less harsh and derisive.

The result of the MRI ruled out a diagnosis of tumor. The doctor was able to prescribe some medication for the migraines. Vechra agreed to try this, so Trudi took her to the pharmacy to fill her prescriptions. The trip to the pharmacy had a dual purpose. Its explicit function was to get Vechra her medicine. The trip also gave Trudi a chance to spend time with Vechra, to talk with her, to analyze her English level for future placement with a tutor, to build a trusting relationship, and to give Trudi a context in which to understand Vechra's concerns and interests. They walked around the pharmacy while waiting for the prescription to be filled, bought mittens for Vechra's children, and looked at books. Trudi found out Vechra had dry skin so they got some lotion.

The caustic, unsympathetic demeanor of the Hospital A doctor, compounding the discomfort of the physical exam, so thoroughly alienated Vechra that she decided to return to her neighborhood doctor without discussing her decision with Trudi or Choulie. In mid-March, during a follow-up appointment at Hospital A, Vechra told Choulie that she had visited a neighborhood doctor for her most recent complaint, a stomachache. This doctor also does not speak her language, but unlike the Hospital A physician, he did not bother her with numerous questions and an uncomfortable examination. Vechra acted out her pain, motioning to her stomach. The doctor gave her a bottle of pills and sent her to another office for X-rays. He gave no explanation of the results of the X-rays, and he offered no follow-up care. This treatment seemed less than thorough to Trudi, who encouraged Vechra to give the medicine prescribed by the Hospital A doctor a chance and see if it would help her. It was obvious that Vechra was not easily going to accept Western forms of medical treatment if they were intimidating or not yielding immediate results. Trudi convinced Vechra to take the migraine medicine prescribed by the Hospital A doctor, and her headaches eventually did subside.

During a follow-up exam at Hospital A on 31 March, with the same doctor that had been demeaning before, Vechra complained of some vaginal discomforts. Without conducting a pelvic exam, he decided that there was nothing sufficiently wrong to warrant sending cultures to the lab. Vechra's complaints persisted, so Trudi offered to get her a new doctor in mid-April. After so many disagreeable encounters with the Hospital A doctor, and considering the gynecological nature of many of Vechra's problems, Trudi decided to switch to a female doctor who happened to be at Hospital B, where it was possible to get an appointment fairly quickly.

Vechra was not ready when Choulie came to pick her up, and consequently they arrived late to the hospital and were not able to see her new doctor. They rescheduled the appointment once again, this time for the first week of May. For her next doctor's visit, Vechra was ready and waiting outside her apartment to be picked up by Choulie and Trudi. It turned out that Vechra had a pelvic inflammatory disease, a yeast infection, and a urinary tract infection, and she was given several prescriptions for antibiotics. Clearly she was in an extremely uncomfortable situation, yet her previous doctor had not done an internal exam.

In early June, Trudi asked Choulie to find out how Vechra was feeling since she had not called the office in a while. When Choulie asked, Vechra said she did not call because she felt good now, and she sounded happy to Choulie. The teacher also noticed increased involvement and support from Vechra in the classes, and she had not voiced further complaints about her headaches. Early in the summer Trudi ran into Vechra and her family at a Cambodian festival being held at the Field Museum. Vechra excitedly greeted Trudi and introduced her to her husband as the person who had helped her deal with her medical problems. The fact that Vechra had gone on an excursion with her children was a sign to Trudi of Vechra's dramatic improvement.

Vechra and her husband are now able to call on Choulie or Trudi when a problem arises, which she did not do in the beginning of their contact with her. Vechra is also showing some autonomy in getting herself to the newly established local Chicago Health Organization clinic, encouraged by the fact that Choulie is one of the clinic translators. The clinic has a designated day for Cambodians to receive care and is within walking distance of Vechra's home.

Choulie, on her part, through accompanying Trudi on her trips with clients to doctor's appointments, is learning how to talk with clients about their health, what questions to ask, and how to manage the bureaucratic aspects of seeing a doctor. Choulie has taken on primary responsibility for getting Vechra appropriate medical care. She keeps Trudi updated on Vechra's condition and progress.

Staff Considerations When Deciding How to Work with a Family

The story of the RFP's work with Vechra points up many of the important factors staff consider when helping a client find appropriate health care. These considerations guide RFP staff's strategies in getting their clients healthy, while gradually moving the clients closer to being able to manage their own health and the health of all their family members.

1. *The medical problem:* Vechra had severe headaches and partial paralysis.
2. *Staff's relationship with the family:* Vechra was initially reluctant to talk about her health problems. Eventually Vechra opened up to the staff.
3. *Available medical resources:* Hospital A seemed the best choice for dealing with the presenting symptoms.
4. *Family characteristics:* There are five family characteristics that staff tries to take into account when deciding how to interpret and respond to a family's medical needs, as shown in the following chart with reference to Vechra.

1. Knowledge and acceptance of Western medicine

a. Awareness of and willingness to report medical problems.	Vechra was at first reluctant to report her health concerns to the program.
b. Knowledge of medical resources	Vechra did not know about any medical resources other than her ineffectual neighborhood doctor.
c. Familiarity with medical procedures	Vechra was completely unfamiliar with Western medical procedures such as the physical exam and MRI.
d. Knowledge of Western medical theory	Vechra had little or no knowledge of Western medicine.

e. Acceptance of Western medicine	Vechra resisted Western medicine at first, but then saw its benefits and became more accepting.
2. Fears and sensitivities	Vechra was frightened by her experiences at Hospital A.
3. English proficiency	Vechra spoke almost no English and so required the help of a translator.
4. Time and energy	Vechra had little time or energy because of her three young children.
5. Material resources	Vechra did not have a driver's license, did not know how to take public transportation, and did not have enough money to take a cab to a doctor.

A Second Case Study is that of Peach.

Peach, His Shot Finger, and the Ash-Soaked Bandage
Kuntheary arrived for Trudi's adult English class one evening seeming very distraught about something. After class Trudi inquired what was the matter and found out Kuntheary was worried about her son Peach who had accidentally shot his finger while playing with a neighbor's gun. Oeun, Kuntheary's mother-in-law, had refused to allow Peach to go to the hospital, saying it would cost too much. Oeun was also worried about reporting the gun to the police.

After English class Trudi went with Kuntheary to see how Peach was doing. She arrived to find him with his finger wrapped in a bandage that had been soaked in urine and ashes. The grandmother, Oeun, had though she could take care of her grandson's wound by using her own traditional method of treatment. Trudi realized this was not an appropriate treatment and explained to the family the urgency of getting Peach more appropriate care and why the urine and ash bandage was not adequate.

Kuntheary stayed home with her other children, and Trudi drove Peach to a nearby hospital where he had immediate surgery on his finger. According to Peach's doctor, he would have had serious medical problems if he had not come to the hospital right away as he did. For Trudi, this incident was a reminder that money issues combined with a domineering, traditional grandmother created regular problems for the family.

Peach was given a prescription for antibiotics, and follow-up appointments were scheduled with the doctor and physical therapy. However, because the health insurance from Kuntheary's husband's job provided only minimal coverage, the family was worried that they could not afford the hospital bill and had Peach discharged early.

After a police report was made at the hospital, Trudi informed the family about where to turn in the unregistered gun. Because the owner of the gun had a bad reputation in the neighborhood and Trudi did not want to have any contact with him, she decided to limit her involvement to helping with the medical problems.

Darin, Kuntheary's husband, and Oeun (Darin's mother) did not want to spend money on Peach's medication or physical therapy. Kuntheary, on the other hand, was worried about Peach and felt the medicine and follow-up were very important for him. She was so committed to this that she personally accompanied Peach to his follow-up appointment because she did not believe he was going to go. Trudi helped Kuntheary work out a payment plan with the hospital for the balance of the surgery bill and gave her some client assistance money to pay for medicine. Peach's finger healed, but because Darin did not believe that physical therapy was required, Peach now has limited use of his finger.

Staff Considerations in the Case of Peach

1. *The medical problem:* Peach's shot finger was an emergency requiring immediate medical attention. The traditional cure employed by his grandmother was potentially harmful.
2. *Staff relationship with the family:* Trudi had known the family for a long time and was able to pick up on Kuntheary's anxiety during their English class. Kuntheary immediately expressed her concerns for her son to Trudi.
3. *Available medical resources:* Hospital B was very close to the Sim family and could treat Peach with emergency surgery.
4. *Family characteristics:* Family characteristics are displayed in the following chart.

    1. Knowledge and acceptance of Western medicine

a. Awareness of and willingness to report medical problems	Kuntheary was worried and thought her son's finger needed medical attention and told Trudi about it. Ouen, the grandmother, however, did not know the wound needed emergency medical attention.
b. Knowledge of medical resources	Kuntheary did not know to take Peach to the emergency room.
c. Familiarity with medical procedures	N/A
d. Knowledge of Western medical theory	This family did not understand the potentially hazardous effects of not keeping an open wound clean. They also did not realize it was necessary for Peach to have surgery and physical therapy to maintain the use of his finger.

e. Acceptance of Western medicine	Kuntheary was very accepting of Western medicine and believed surgery and the medicines and physical therapy were necessary for the well-being of her son. Darin and Oeun, on the other hand, were not as accepting.
2. Fears and sensitivities	Peach was afraid of the police because of his involvement with an illegal gun.
3. English proficiency	Kuntheary had limited knowledge of English and was not comfortable speaking English. Trudi's help was needed in communicating the problem to the doctor and relating his instructions to Kuntheary and Peach.
4. Time and energy	Kuntheary has seven children and her husband is not responsive to his children's needs, so Trudi took Peach to the doctor herself and let Kuntheary stay home with her other children.
5. Material resources	The family is very poor and their medical insurance did not take care of much of the cost of Peach's treatment. The program provided the family with a small grant and helped them figure out how to pay the hospital bills on a monthly basis.

The strategies used in getting Peach's finger taken care of were: being available to Kuntheary's concerns; investigating the problem and assessing what medical help was needed; impressing upon the family that the problem was serious and required medical attention; driving the child to the doctor; explaining the situation to Kuntheary; explaining the directions for follow-up treatment; and providing them with a way to pay for the medical bills. A primary principle that Trudi followed in Peach's case was that of persistence. She did not accept the grandmother's decision to treat Peach herself. Instead she advocated Kuntheary's position, who wanted her son to get medical care.

Diagnosis: Finding Out about Medical Problems

On Trudi's first visit with a family, she describes the features of the RFP program and what services are available to participating families. Included in this description, of course, is the topic of health care. As part of this first visit Trudi or the bilingual home visitor will usually inquire about the family members' health. They try to get a sense of their medical history and ask if they have had or are currently receiving care from a particular physician, clinic, or hospital. They find out if anyone in the family is currently taking medicine and may ask to see the medicine in order to have a better idea of what health problems the client may have and who their doctor has been. There have been times when RFP staff have discovered critical situations such as a client taking a prescribed drug incorrectly. In other instances Trudi has found out about children who were not receiving prescribed follow-up treatment for very serious conditions.

In addition to problems that are already being tended to in some fashion, the family service staff or the teacher will ask very specific questions about clients' health to find out if a medical problem is being ignored. Often a client will repeatedly report that they are feeling fine even if he or she has been experiencing chronic pain.

Keen observation is another essential element in the home visitor's bag of health problem investigative tricks. One can learn a lot about the status of a family's health just by paying attention to how they look. Are the children flushed? Do they have runny noses? Is the mother lethargic? Are there obvious physical impairments like limps or droopy eyes? Is someone sporting a makeshift bandage? Clues such as these provide RFP staff with specifics to ask about, often resulting in more detailed, specific responses.

Finally, all RFP teachers and bilingual workers inquire about the reason for a student's absence from a class to find out during a home visit why a parent or older child is home from work or school. If the cause is an illness, they find out if it is serious enough to require medical attention and help them arrange an appointment.

In summary, some useful ways to find out about client health problems are (1) ask general or specific questions about family health; (2) ask specific questions about any medicine being taken and examine medicines; (3) be observant; and (4) investigate illness as possible reason for child's or parent's absence from class.

Mapping Medical Options

The process of facilitating effective health connections for families requires, ideally, developing knowledge of and relationships with a set of quality medical service institutions that can meet families' needs. The RFP relies primarily on nine medical facilities in Chicago with which they establish relationships for their clients. The question is, how do they choose which of Chicago's medical facilities they will place on their map of preferred medical options?

There are seven basic criteria that guide their selection of these facilities:

1. *Quality of care:* High quality of medical service.
2. *Distance from refugee neighborhood:* The closer the medical facility is to the client's house, the better.
3. *Continuity:* RFP staff ideally want their clients to be associated with one institution and one doctor for their continuous general care.
4. *Receptivity to refugee patients:* Translators on staff, acceptance of patients on public aid without discrimination, overall friendliness, respect for patients, and willingness to set appointments for a reasonably close time.
5. *Female doctors:* Staff has found that the female refugee clients always prefer women doctors.

6. *Medical specialization:* Some of the clients' medical problems require specialized treatment for things such as asthma, post-traumatic stress disorder, and gynecologic problems.
7. *Age specialization:* The hospital is fully equipped to deal with a particular age group, e.g., children.

Neighborhood Doctors Who Practice Western Medicine
There are three neighborhood doctors whom many of the refugee families visit because they are close and often employ translators. In RFP staff's estimation the quality of care provided by these doctors is not adequate. Examples of inadequate care include: prescribing drugs without making a diagnosis based on physical examination and medical history, not releasing medical records, unsanitary office conditions, unlawful billing practices, and lack of follow-up care.

Herbal Practitioners
Refugees often go to a Chinese herbalist and talk to the person behind the counter, asking what to take for various medical conditions. RFP staff does not discourage this kind of medicine. Rather, they try to help clients think about the limits of traditional medicine and whether they would be better off supplementing the treatment with Western care. They try to make sure that when their clients talk to a Western doctor they are honest and open about what other kinds of remedies they are taking.

Progress and Health: How Families Improve on the Medical Connectedness Scale

Presenting symptoms, available medical resources, family characteristics, and the nature of the relationship between client and the RFP staff are all taken into account when working with a family on medical issues.

Recently, the RFP has developed a "medical connectedness scale" that charts a family's position and progress in relation to their ability and propensity to find and utilize adequate health care (see appendix C). Some of these dimensions have been discussed above as part of family character-istics. The five dimensions of the scale are as follows.

1. *Awareness of medical needs with motive to act:* Before a fam-ily can begin to actually receive medical care, they have to realize that they need it. Therefore, a first step in con-necting families with medical resources is teaching them to pay attention to their own health, as well as teaching parents how to be vigilant over their children's health by constantly asking pointed questions about the health of all family members when they make home visits.

2. *Understanding of Western medicine:* The objective is to provide clients with basic explanations that provide a basis for understanding issues such as the importance of sterile conditions when dealing with open wounds and the necessity of taking a complete prescription of antibiotics. Some other lessons RFP staff try to teach cen-ter on issues of interacting with doctors, dealing with insurance companies, and keeping track of personal records.

3. *Acceptance of Western medicine and willingness to engage adequate medical resources:* An attitude of suspicion is an understandable and common reaction to something that is unfamiliar. Many families enter the program with a low score on this dimension, and it takes a calmly persuasive demeanor on the part of the RFP staff to help families gain confidence in the Western medical system.

4. *Ability to access adequate medical resources with the help of program staff:* This fourth dimension concerns how well a family can put together the three previous dimensions so as to be able to recognize when a medical problem requires attention and to entrust their child's or their own health to a physician.

5. *Autonomy:* A family's ultimate independence in con-necting to high-quality medical assistance is the long-term goal toward which the previous four dimensions point.

8 Language Instruction for Parents

The primary goal of language instruction for parents is to encourage proficiency in English as part of the plan to help families function better. The Refugee Families Program (RFP) aims to meet this goal by providing English instruction in several contexts.

The ability or inability to speak English plays a critical role in the overall adaptation of refugee families. Forced to leave their homelands, many refugees lose a sense of efficacy and self-definition. The loss is greatly exacerbated by an inability to speak the language of their new country. A failure to speak English not only isolates refugees from the institutions of their new society but often serves to isolate parents from their children.

By providing English instruction, the RFP aims to increase the self-sufficiency of the parents. When parents can speak some English, they can manage a significant number of functions without staff help. For example, the improved English of one of the mothers allowed her to go to the hospital for lab tests unaccompanied by a staff member. Speaking English also improves the position in the family of some parents by reducing their dependence on their children to translate for them. Being able to communicate in English gives a boost to parents' self-esteem and further motivates them to work at adapting to their new environment.

Objectives for each participant's English instruction are set by the instructor. At the time of entry into the RFP, Trudi discusses with the parents their interest in pursuing English instruction. If they profess an interest, she assesses their proficiency in English, has a bilingual worker assess their literacy level in their native language, and together with the bilingual worker evaluates their motivation in order to determine what kind of instruction would best fit their needs.

Other variables that affect both the approach and the objectives are

- The relationship of the native language alphabet to Western script
- Age of the parent
- Urban or rural background
- Length of time in this country (involving recent arrivals in English instruction is easier than engaging those who have been in the country longer.)
- Number of children at home and in school
- Cultural value of education (especially for women)
- Family health
- Level of family stability
- Literacy resources in the family's support system (if relatives speak and read English, the parent may be less motivated to learn a new language)

Another important factor that affects a parent's motivation to learn a new language is his or her mode of adaptation to American culture. In general, there are three modes of adaptation: holding tightly to traditional values and practices; eagerly assimilating oneself and one's family into the American mainstream; and taking on a bicultural identity, preserving traditional values while acquiring some new values and practices in order to be successful in American society.

English instruction for parents takes place in several contexts:

1. *Child-parent classes:* As described in chapter 3, parents become familiar with terms, vocabulary, and expressions that would be found in a common preschool setting. Children and parents are exposed to many children's books that supplement their vocabulary.
2. *Group instruction:* English instruction for groups of parents takes place in one of the parents' apartments. It is taught by volunteers. Group instruction is the

best context for three or four mothers who live in the same apartment building or live nearby.

3. *One-on-one instruction:* Instruction takes place in the parent's home and is taught by a volunteer or a teacher. One-on-one instruction is provided to parents at all levels of English proficiency.
4. *Outside sources:* English as a Second Language classes are held in community colleges, park districts, and community centers. Parents can be referred to any of these outside sources at any point in their participation in the program. If a referral is to be made, the parent must have time to attend one of the classes and the confidence to venture into the outside learning situation.

Mai is an Amerasian who received no schooling in Vietnam. During a period of several years she received English instruction at home through the RFP. She made good progress, improving her "survival" English. The year her son went to kindergarten, the RFP staff approached Mai with the idea of going to classes at the community college. She was reticent at first and was afraid Lisa, her teacher, would no longer work with her at home. She was assured that Lisa would continue, and Trudi encourage Mai to sign up for the afternoon classes that met four times a week. Trudi felt that Mai's English would improve faster with more classes and she would be less likely to feel defeated.

After a few months, Mai reported that she liked the teacher at the college and that she felt good about the classes. Mai's self-confidence was greatly improved, and she was no longer nervous about attending school. A few years ago, when Mai was first approached about attending class, she was too anxious and did not wish to go. She also had babysitting problems. But after some time with a tutor, when she knew some basic English and her child care problems were solved, she was ready for this new experience. Being ready for classes is always an important issue when referring parents to outside sources.

Phases of Language Instruction

English instruction conducted by the RFP, whether in a small group or one-on-one, is based on Escabar and McKeon's (1979) concept that lessons are provided in four phases.

Phase 1: Establishing Meaning

This phase is most critical for parents who have minimal English skills. They are, by far, the largest group represented in the RFP program. For these parents (often mothers) the objective is to orient lessons around life skills. The content of phase 1 lessons centers on survival English and basic communication skills, such as "How are you?" and "My name is Dao." In this phase parents also begin to learn to write their names, addresses, telephone numbers, and Social Security numbers. The instructors find that the use of tangible objects, such as an apple or glass, is one way of establishing meaning. Photographs and actions, such as walking, running, and so on, are other ways.

The instructor has the responsibility for making all the vocabulary used in the lesson clear. Repetition of words or phrases is not enough; the parent must understand their meaning. Because of the importance of this phase, Trudi stresses to the instructors that they move slowly through the first lessons with the parents.

Four Cambodian mothers were grouped together to work with a volunteer English instructor. They were all illiterate in their native language. Therefore, lesson plans focused on survival English, emphasizing speaking and verbal comprehension. Writing was very difficult for these mothers, so it was kept simple (alphabet, simple numbers, names, addresses, and Social Security numbers).

The instructor found children's books to be very helpful, particularly Dr. Seuss books that used rhyming words. As the year progressed, the instructor found it necessary to provide individualized instruction. One mother's attendance was irregular because of marital difficulties. Another mother had a child with severe medical problems, which made it hard for her to focus on learning English. For these two mothers instruction moved slowly, and they remained in phase 1 for the year.

The other two mothers were able to practice their new skills with their school-aged children, and their learning proceeded more rapidly. They were both able to move into phase 2 toward the end of the school year, where they could practice written exercises and engage in more complex dialogue.

Phase 2: Practice

Phase 2 parents may be able to speak some English, but they cannot read or write. For these parents, the focus goes beyond survival English to increasing their speaking and verbal comprehension. Simple reading and writing are included.

Phase 1 and phase 2 parents need a great deal of practice. Instructors ensure that practice is meaningful, which makes the repetition less boring and encourages parents to practice on their own. Communicative practice helps parents move from the classroom to outside environments.

In phase 2, instructors continue to move slowly, staying away from complicated grammar skills or difficult reading and writing. To keep classes interesting, instructors continue to focus on meaningful language content, such as food, clothing, family, and transportation.

Dac was a Vietnamese mother who had received formal training in nursing, and her literacy level in her native language was good. Both her verbal and her written English were minimal, but she was very motivated to learn the language. Because she was unable to attend a scheduled class, she was provided with an individual instructor who came to her apartment.

Her instructor started her out with basic survival English. Dac's motivation was high, and she absorbed the material quickly. Furthermore, the Vietnamese alphabet uses Western letters and is phonetic, making English less difficult for her.

Her instructor soon learned that speaking, verbal comprehension, and simple writing were not challenging enough for Dac, and she added grammar exercises and a journal. The journal combined expressing herself in English with grammar lessons. Dac applied herself to learning English and practiced with her school-aged children and her husband. Dac moved quickly through phase 1 and was able to combine the more purposeful communication of phases 2 and 3 within the year.

Phase 3: Parent Initiated Communication
In this phase, the parent moves out of the practice mode into using more purposeful communication. The content is parent-initiated, manipulating and recombining what has already been taught and integrating new patterns and vocabulary learned outside of the teaching situation.

Vong, a Vietnamese father, requested individual instruction so that he could progress faster and concentrate on his pronunciation, which was poor. Vong had received formal education in Vietnam studying law, and had the equivalent of a bachelor's degree in the United States. Vong's self-esteem was low owing in part to his inability to use his education in the United States. The staff was concerned about him and hoped that additional English instruction might help his overall adaptation.

Although Vong was suffering from post-traumatic stress disorder, which took its toll on his energy, he was determined to succeed in this country and was very motivated to learn. He particularly wanted to learn about the real estate field and purchased some books that he brought to his tutoring sessions. The instructor felt conflicted because she feared the books might be too difficult for Vong and she wanted him to experience success. Furthermore, she was afraid she was playing into his fantasies about a career that might not be realizable.

However, because of the importance of meaningful instruction, the instructor decided to integrate the real estate books into the lessons. To her relief, because of Vong's legal knowledge, he was able to connect to many of the concepts in real estate. The instructor used the material to teach Vong how to read more difficult paragraphs, looking at key words to get the main idea of the material. Other resources were added, including children's novels and newspapers, and idioms were stressed in the lessons. Vong did well; his English improved and so did his self-esteem.

Phase 4: Review, Recombination, or Reteaching
This phase reviews all lessons and helps parents with content that needs to be taught again. This phase emphasizes higher-level English skills including reading and writing.

Selecting English Instructors

English instruction is provided by volunteers and RFP teaching staff and occasionally by ESL professionals, when budget allows.

The program director is very careful in selecting the instructors and in matching them with parents. The volunteers may not know very much about the families in the beginning, but it is vital that they learn about and appreciate the families' personal histories, cultural heritage, and values. Knowing about the traumas that have been experienced and understanding the norms of interpersonal behavior, religious observances, and the hierarchy of family structure help instructors work effectively with parents. (For further details on orientation of personnel, see chapters 9 and 10.)

Part C: Program Administration

9 Teachers and Bilingual Staff: Recruitment, Training, and Supervision

What kinds of background and human qualities characterize people who function well as teachers or bilingual staff? How are they recruited, trained, supported, and supervised?

The Teachers

The primary role of the teachers, as we have seen in chapters 3 and 4, is to provide structure, stimulation, guidance, and support to the child-parent preschool classes that meet twice a week, mainly in the apartments of participating families. Teachers may also provide child development assistance or language instruction to individual families who, for one reason or another, do not fit into the regular multifamily child-parent classes (see chapter 3). In the context of doing their job, the teachers are asked to become keen observers of the participating parents and children, to be continually aware of health or other problems in the family that might be addressed through the family service component.

Characteristics of Successful Teachers in the Refugee Program
    From the program director's standpoint, successful teachers in the Refugee Families Program (RFP) share the following characteristics.

1. *Interested in different cultures and peoples:* Most often, the teachers in the program have had experience in the Peace Corps or similar in-depth exposure to another

Lisa, a teacher, gives special attention to two young children.

culture. They come to the program with a considerable degree of cultural sensitivity.

2. *Interested in working with both children and adults, not just one or the other.*

3. *Observant and perceptive, able to pick up on nonverbal cues:* This is especially important in this situation, where one is working with people who do not speak one's own language.

4. *Flexible and creative:* The teacher goes into class and does not know exactly what will happen since it occurs in people's homes. Someone may be present that the teacher has not anticipated; for example, an older sibling or a neighbor. She needs to shape her class to include them. In another instance, the teacher may have planned an inside activity, but because it is a beautiful day the group wants to go outside. She has to be able to adjust. If the class is working with numbers there are plenty of things to count outside. If they are studying body parts there are myriad opportunities to engage in body movement in the outside setting that point up

particular parts and movements of the body. On an ongoing basis, it is the teacher's task to build in some of the unexpected and surprising to accompany the stable, repetitive structure of the classes. Teachers with a more rigid style of teaching may be excellent in other settings, but not in the setting of the child-parent classes.

5. *Well organized:* Given that the class lasts only one and one-half hours and takes place away from the teacher's source of materials, she has to think clearly about what she will need in class on a particular day. Further, the objects that she decides to bring to class must be light enough to carry and be packed in the order in which she will use them.

6. *Willing to share and communicate with the other teachers:* Repeatedly, the program has found that teachers enrich and improve each other's teaching by sharing their strengths and innovations in curriculum development.

7. *Ideally, experienced in teaching preschool age children and well grounded in the developmental stages in young children.*

In general, the teachers in the program have been in their early or middle twenties. All have B.A. or M.A. degrees. For the most part, on entering the program they were not versed in the particular cultures that they were to encounter in their work. This had to be built into their training.

The single best avenue for finding appropriate teachers has been through college and university placement offices. In one case, a teacher approached the program initially as a volunteer. She showed great promise while serving as a volunteer in the after-school homework classes (see chapter 5) and was taken on as a teacher when an opening occurred.

Training of Program Teachers

Teacher orientation begins with extensive discussion of the refugee situation: how these particular refugees end up in Chicago, what they have gone through, and the different steps they had to take along the way, starting with preparation to escape. This is discussed in the context of their geographical and cultural origins. The orientation then moves on to the nature of the various refugee communities in Chicago and elsewhere.

Most of the Cambodian refugee adults served by the RFP and some of the Vietnamese refugees, especially the former political prisoners, suffer from some form of post-traumatic stress disorder (PTSD). Teachers need to have a good understanding of PTSD symptoms and their origin. For example, PTSD symptoms frequently include nightmares, nervousness, inability to focus, depression, impaired memory, loss of appetite, and a sense that nothing matters. As these symptoms may be reflected in the parents' behavior in class, they need to be understood and embraced.

It is important that teachers understand the ways in which the refugee families' lives can be complicated severely by ongoing connections with relatives in the country of origin. Life can become painfully complicated if a family is receiving letters or collect calls suddenly requesting money to deal with illness, death, or other family crises. These requests can result easily in a parent's emotional withdrawal from a child or in a diversion of funds set aside for food or clothing for the children. While the well-being of family abroad is a critical concern for parents, these relationships are next to meaningless for the children, who in most cases have never met these relatives.

The best qualifications a teacher can have for relating with the refugee families are overall respect for others and sensitivity. The teachers are encouraged to pick up on feelings and to trust their instincts regarding what are right and wrong actions and responses. Within this overall posture, there are a number of concrete cultural differences for which teachers can be prepared:

1. Do not insist on a handshake or other physical connection when you meet family members.
2. Do not insist that family members look you in the eye. Their skewed glance may be a sign of respect.
3. Keep your voice at a low level, not boisterous, loud, or brash.

4. Take your shoes off when entering a home and leave them just inside the door, especially when it is clear that this is the family's custom.
5. Understand that both children and adults may need time for warming up to your presence in their home. Give them space. Do not insist that they fully engage with you on first encounter.
6. If offered something to eat or drink, express your gratitude and take at least one bite or sip. Don't leave it untouched.
7. Be prepared to sit on the floor with family members.
8. When sitting on the floor, be sure to have your legs tucked under or curled (Southeast Asian and African women both sit that way).
9. Dress modestly, and do not wear things that draw attention to your body; e.g., do not wear tight clothes or shorts.

Supervision of Teachers

The supervision of teachers by the program director takes place during daily conversations with the two teachers. Teachers normally are in the office an hour each morning prior to class and an hour each afternoon and all day Friday. They use this time to prepare and write their daily class reports. The desks of the two teachers and the director are all in the same intimate space. This arrangement encourages the ongoing discussion of concrete classroom issues. The discussion may focus on a teacher's concerns about the way she presented a particular concept or activity. It may focus on interactions among children (e.g., two children who are not getting along well) or on the difficulties of a particular child who is fearful and withdrawn. These informal interactions also provide the context in which teachers can report observations that suggest some kind of follow-up by the director and/or a bilingual worker, e.g., the illness of a parent or child, the apparent pregnancy of a mother, or adjustment difficulties of a particular child who can be helped through the gentle intervention of a bilingual worker. In this manner, the ongoing process of sharing in the office provides a vital nexus through which the director can gather information on the families and transmit the teachers' perceptions to the bilingual workers.

A critical factor in this highly effective process of supervision is the physical availability and proximity of the director. For this reason the director has refused an offer from the agency to have her own separate office down the hall.

Teacher Collaboration

As with all good teaching, ample planning time is crucial. A full planning day every Friday gives the two teachers a chance to learn from each other and profit from each other's strengths. For example, one teacher is strong in the area of music while another is strong in ideas for three-dimension visual art. The teachers can also benefit in their planning from the work of previous program teachers by consulting the card index file that organizes children's activities by curriculum themes. In turn, the current teachers continually add to this file as they develop new activities.

Bilingual Staff

The primary role of the bilingual workers is in the family service component, as described in chapters 6 and 7 above. Their job is to listen carefully to the needs and sensitivities of the families to which they are assigned, to communicate their perceptions to the rest of the staff, and to be major cultural brokers in the relationships between the families and the range of institutions on which they are dependent for their well-being. They also participate in the after-school homework classes (chapter 5) and may sometimes be involved in one-to-one cognitive development work with a mother and child in cases where families do not join the regular child-parent classes (see chapter 2).

The addition of the bilingual workers in the fourth year of the program (1993–94) brought about an important deepening of communication between program staff as a whole and the families they serve. The roles of teacher and bilingual worker are highly complementary. Each completes the work of the other, with the director playing the key role of guiding, connecting, and supplementing the work of both.

Three part-time bilingual workers are currently on staff. Nancy Tran is Vietnamese, in her late twenties, and arrived in the United States in her early teens, attending high school in Chicago. Her clients in the program are Vietnamese families, including the Amerasian families (see chapter 1). Choulie Hoc was born and raised in a Chinese family living in an area of Cambodia that borders on Vietnam. As a result she speaks Chinese, Vietnamese, and Khmer (Cambodian). She serves Cambodian, Chinese, and Vietnamese families in the program. Sattha Eap, a Cambodian, is a certified bilingual teacher at the elementary school that serves the majority of the Cambodian families in the program. Her primary role in the RFP is to assist in the after-school homework class (see chapter 5).

Characteristics of Successful Bilingual Workers

The characteristics shared by successful bilingual workers are similar to those exhibited by successful teachers.

1. *Observant and perceptive.*
2. *Interested and warm, having a genuine liking for people.*
3. *Nonjudgmental:* This is an attribute that is particularly salient in the selection of bilingual workers. Given that they tend to be more educated and from a higher social stratum in their country of origin than most of the clients whom they serve in the program, there is the ever-present possibility that a candidate for a bilingual position can carry into the job attitudes of class superiority. This must be carefully considered in the recruitment interviews.
4. *Willing to admit what they don't know.*
5. *Open to working as a team member:* They do not take a go-it-alone, proprietary attitude toward their work with clients.
6. *Well respected in the refugee community.*
7. *Relatively free from identification with particular vested interests or factions in their community.* For example, it

is vital that the worker not be perceived by clients as identified with a religious or political group that contributes to polarization within the refugee community.

Training of Bilingual Workers

The initial orientation for bilingual workers includes an introduction to the goals and procedures of the program along with extensive discussions on the nature of the institutions to which the workers will be playing a bridging role for the clients. The importance of confidentiality is stressed, since being part of their respective refugee communities means the bilingual workers are particularly vulnerable to making inadvertent slips. The orientation process also becomes an integral part of ongoing supervision by the program director as the bilingual worker engages in her work with families.

Supervision of Bilingual Workers

Supervision of bilingual workers, like that of teachers, takes places informally, in the context of ongoing discourse on the work with particular families. The desks of the bilingual workers are in the same space with those of the teachers and the program director. Bilingual workers are in the office, writing reports, receiving assignments, and discussing their work with the director several times a week. Additional communications between the program director and the bilingual workers take place on the telephone.

Collaboration with Teachers

Ongoing collaboration between bilingual workers and teachers is essential to a high quality of functioning in the RFP. The bilingual workers not only understand the clients culturally and speak their language, but are also privy to helpful information about the clients that comes through the community grapevine. They are the only ones capable of in-depth communication with the families concerning the families' problems, needs, and perceptions. They help interpret enigmatic behavior to the teachers. They will often attend the child-parent classes, especially in the early phases of a cycle, in order to ease some client's entry into the class and build relationships with parents that can lead to assistance to the family in other areas such as medical care. In order for this collaboration to function smoothly, bilingual workers and teachers need to think of themselves and behave as an integrally connected team. The program director, as we shall see in chapter 11, plays a key role in facilitating this collaborative process.

10 Volunteers: Recruitment, Training, Supervision, and Functions

At any one time there are about five volunteers working with families in the program. They are mostly involved in teaching English to parents in the parents' homes, either on a one-to-one basis or working with a small group. Volunteers may also work with young children in the home or assist in the after-school homework classes. Frequently volunteers will start their work with a family in a limited way, such as language instruction, and then gradually expand their relationship with the family to include trips to the zoo, to the parks, or to shopping locations that the family would not ordinarily visit.

The volunteer program has been eminently successful. Its inclusion of only five volunteers at a time is due primarily to limited RFP resources for volunteer recruitment, training, and supervision. The program director estimates that virtually every mother in the RFP would want in-home English instruction if it were available, especially during weekdays when the mothers tend to be free.

Who Are the Volunteers and How Are They Recruited?

The volunteers tend to be women. They also tend to have B.A. degrees or to be in B.A. college programs.

Volunteers come to the RFP through a variety of channels. Some call the agency (Travelers & Immigrants Aid) looking for a volunteer opportunity and are passed on to the program by the agency's volunteer coordinator. Others respond to an

A volunteer helps three boys in the after-school class.

announcement of internships posted by the program in university placement offices. Others hear about the program through friends who are already serving as volunteers.

Attributes of Successful Volunteers

The personal attributes of the most successful volunteers tend to be the following:

1. *Clearly motivated to form a helping connection with a family as an end in itself:* The program director will not accept a volunteer if the relationship is viewed by the volunteer as a means to an end (e.g., for religious proselytization).
2. *Truly interested in people, in addition to wanting to teach a specific subject.*
3. *Nonjudgmental.*
4. *Able to gain a basic sense of satisfaction from the experience of the relationship itself:* They do not need to get a large amount of support and recognition from the program director or other RFP staff.

5. *Reasonably confident about entering strange situations.*
6. *Flexible:* they do not need to keep a rigid schedule or to have highly predictable situations.

The Screening Process

In order to explore some of the above dimensions with a prospective volunteer, the program director frequently presents a number of challenging scenarios in the screening interview process. For example:

- "What would you do if when you arrived at the apartment building you found that the doorbell didn't work?"
- "How would you feel if you saw mice running around the room where you were teaching?"
- "What would you do if you arrived to find the family in the middle of eating their dinner?"
- "What would you do if on arriving at the apartment you found that a child was very ill?"

Often the volunteers self-select out of the running in response to these simple probes. They know that this type of situation would not work for them. Other applicants may not withdraw, but their answers are not sufficiently convincing to warrant accepting them in the volunteer role. The most promising candidates are those who tend to see these scenarios as genuinely interesting and possibly challenging.

The key attribute embracing all the others is the volunteer's capacity to form a relationship with the client that is underpinned by trust and ease of communication. As a rule of thumb, if you as an interviewer have difficulty trusting the candidate, even if you cannot say precisely why, it would not be advisable to take him or her on as a volunteer.

Matching of Volunteers to Families

Once a candidate has been accepted as a volunteer, the next step is to create a proper match with a family. The object is to create a fit between what the family wants and what the volunteer wants. If a parent has an obsessive need for certainty and tranquility, then a volunteer must be found who is 100 percent reliable and who speaks softly and quietly. If a volunteer wants a broad, open, friendly relationship with a family, not formally confined to a language-teaching role, then find a family whose style and desires match those motives in the volunteer. On the other hand, some volunteers want to confine the relationship to a more formal, narrowly defined function. Families can be found who are most comfortable with that type of connection. The occasional male volunteer is always matched with male clients.

Orientation, Supervision, and Support

Volunteers need to be oriented to the cultural and historical dimensions of their client families in much the same way as the teachers need to be oriented (see chapter 9). They often will need to be introduced to the safety precautions to be taken in operating in the family's neighborhood. Volunteers who are going to be teaching English as a second language are introduced to the materials in the program office that can assist them with the ESL process. The program director may also put them in touch with one of the ESL teachers at the local junior college.

After a volunteer has been working with a family for several weeks, the program director or one of the bilingual workers will call the family to see how the new relationship is going or will ask in the context of doing other work with the family. The program director also talks with the volunteers after each of the first few sessions. Subsequent checks with both the family and the volunteer take place periodically during the ensuing months.

There is no formal supervisory arrangement for volunteers. They call the program director when they want to talk. It is essential that the program director be available for these calls. The volunteer is not likely to last long in the role if he or she feels isolated and alone. The program director gives her home number to volunteers in order to enhance this availability.

Thus far we have examined three primary requirements in the selection and maintenance of a successful volunteer: (1) the proper personal attributes; (2) a proper match between volunteer and family; and (3) ongoing support as needed. Even after all three requirements have been met, problems requiring some kind of advice and support are likely to arise in the volunteer-client relationship. Many of these can be characterized as "boundary" issues. They include:

1. *Families asking for advice on complex issues, such as domestic violence or sticky financial problems:* Volunteers are counseled to bring these types of issues to their discussion with the program director rather than try to handle them on their own.

2. *Families asking for money or being in such a depressed financial state that the volunteer feels driven to offer monetary assistance:* Sometimes it is appropriate to do so, but often it is inadvisable. The volunteer may need help in making these discernments.

3. *Families extending invitations to the volunteer that entail obligations that the volunteer is not able to meet:* For example, the volunteer may not be able to meet the monetary gift obligation entailed by attendance at a wedding.

4. *The volunteer inviting the family into his or her home:* This often leads to discomfort on both sides, stemming from the discrepancy between the volunteer's home situation and that of the family. As a general rule of thumb, volunteers are discouraged from inviting families to their homes. In the early stages of the relationship they are also advised not to give their telephone number to the family. Communications are made through the program director.

5. *Misunderstanding in the relationship, often arising from differing expectations.*

None of these complications are surprising. They do, however, point up the great importance of quality selection, matching, and ongoing support of volunteers. They also suggest the importance of a seasoned person having the role of volunteer coordinator.

11   Coordination

Currently, the Refugee Families Program (RFP) has service connections with seventy families at least once a month in one or more facets of the RFP. This includes families in the child-parent classes (all of whom are also receiving family service), families receiving one-to-one teaching or other assistance, and families who no longer have children in the classes or in one-to-one instruction but who continue to receive assistance in times of serious need, e.g., medical crises, domestic violence, or trouble with the law. The thirty families involved in the after-school homework classes include some of the above families as well as children of families who are in none of the above categories.

Given the complexities of serving these families, of coordinating staff, and of coordinating services across the different contexts in which the RFP operates, what has been learned about how to make the RFP function as an efficient whole?

In the view of the program director, the essence of program effectiveness lies in the cooperative connectedness among the teachers, the bilingual workers, and the program director. The guiding principle is for everyone to know as much as possible about the RFP as a whole. In a program in which one is working with the whole family and being as responsive as possible to the family in the context of the community, then all staff have to be aware of what is going on across the boards. The individual teachers need to know about each other's classes and families. Without this shared knowledge there would be much less sharing of teaching strategies, experiences, frustrations, and excitement about accomplishments. If one teacher feels that something significant has happened in her class and the other teacher does not know anything about the children, parents, or events, there is less tendency to share and less value acquired through a sharing exchange. Similarly, each bilingual worker needs to know about the child-parent classes in which their assigned families are operating and about the families being served by the other bilingual worker. They in turn need to share information about the families with the teachers. Participation in the homework classes (chapter 5) or access to the events and communications that emerge in those classes is also essential for an effective knowledge base among staff as a whole. In a parallel fashion the program director shares information with the teachers and bilingual workers about issues of RFP functioning and about her direct service work with families. Without this kind of widespread sharing of information the RFP runs the risk of being fragmented and, hence, less effective. Without it, staff would not only be less informed and less inclined to share experience, but feel less ownership of and investment in the program as a whole. Therefore, one of the key jobs of coordination is to keep the lines of communication open.

The program director, Trudi Langendorf, is the pivotal figure in the coordination process. The role of director involves both administration and direct service. Her direct service role includes four to twelve hours per week in the family service component—visiting families, calling families on the phone, accompanying parents and children to the hospital, etc.—and five hours per week in the after-school homework classes. In her estimation, this direct contact with families, while necessitated by a limited personnel budget, is also essential to both her coordination and her supervision functions. To be separated from families or from the institutions to which they are being connected by the RFP would cut her off from direct knowledge of what families need and how best to deliver RFP services. It also would severely limit her creativity and effectiveness as a supervisor.

In addition to the direct service function, the role of the director includes the following:

1. *Recruitment:* Recruiting families, conducting intake interviews, and setting up child-parent classes and language instruction (see chapter 2); recruiting and training staff and volunteers (chapters 9 and 10).
2. *Supervision of teachers, bilingual workers, and volunteers:* Daily communication with teachers (chapter 9) and frequent communication with volunteers (chapter 10); daily discussion of cases with bilingual workers (in person or on the phone) and setting up specific arrangements to accompany families to appointments with hospitals, clinics, and agencies.
3. *Referrals:* Telephone calls to arrange appointments at hospitals, clinics, schools, Public Aid, subsidized housing, utilities, and other institutions to which the refugee families need to be connected (chapters 6 and 7); contacting these agencies to get information for families or to straighten out misunderstandings and make adjustments, for example, getting a family back on food stamps, providing additional information about a family to a Social Security caseworker who is handling a disability claim, or arranging for a family's heat to be turned back on.
4. *Administration:* Reading ongoing reports of teachers and bilingual staff; writing reports on her own direct service work with families; passing information between teachers and bilingual workers; meeting with Erikson Institute technical assistance and/or documentation/evaluation personnel and coordinating teacher participation in the documentation process, e.g., filling out the child checklists and parent-child checklists twice a year; enrolling child graduates of the child-parent classes in Head Start, day care, or kindergarten; referring families to additional services within TIA/CC, e.g., Mental Health Services, Employment Services, Immigration Services, and substance abuse programs; maintaining ongoing relationships with the spectrum of institutions with which the RFP connects, which often involves calls to key staff with whom the director has not had recent contact but on whom she will eventually rely for cooperation; writing

grant applications and reports (roughly 10 percent of the director's working time).

These myriad coordinating functions of the director take place primarily in three contexts: in the field working with families (her direct service and recruitment roles), in the office conferring with staff, and in the office making telephone calls. She is the hub and facilitator of communication within the program and between the program and the institutions with which the clients are being connected.

Part D: Extending the Work of the Refugee Families Program

12 Considerations in Designing Programs for Refugees and Other Populations

We hope that the concepts and experiences described in chapters 1–11 can be useful in designing and implementing programs for populations, including refugees, who have difficulty supporting the positive development of their children and who find themselves isolated from many of the potentially supportive institutions of the society. As victims of trauma, poverty, and low levels of education these families may include children who do not do well in school, adults who have difficulty finding and holding jobs, or family members whose health is compromised.

This chapter has two parts: Part A presents some of the issues and lessons learned in the course of conducting the Refugee Families Program over a six-year period. It also lists some of the questions that arose and that could be considered by the reader.

Part B presents an eleven-point planning outline for designing programs to serve such families, anticipating that each planner's response to an outline such as this will be distinctly different from another planner's response, depending on the nature of the population each serves, the resources on hand, and the overall mission and priorities of the organization providing the services.

Part A: Issues and Lessons Learned

The overall goal of the Refugee Families Program is to help the participating families gain the skills and self-confidence needed to improve their lives and particularly to support their children's school experience. A major part of this process is to reduce the isolation of these families from the life-supporting institutions that are available in their immediate or larger community.

The following discussion looks at some of the issues and the lessons learned by staff in the process of developing the program. Some of these issues are thorny, require continued reflection, and may only be resolved through major alterations in future program design.

Issue No. 1: Original plans are not always sufficient to meet the key goals of the program and often have to be changed. For example, very early in the program's history, Trudi and the teachers realized that roughly 40 percent of the children were not profiting sufficiently from a 5.5-month, three-hour-a-week program to prepare them adequately for preschool or kindergarten. The staff's first response was to reenroll those children in a second cycle.

By the end of the third year, however, it was obvious that virtually all the children and the parents could profit from a longer experience in the preschool classes. Consequently the classes were extended to 9.5 months, still meeting three hours a week. The remaining two months of each year (July and August) were devoted to outings and special activities that included many parents and older siblings.

The changes aimed at increasing children's schooling experience in the RFP were supported by the RFP's funder, the United Way of Chicago, which recognized the need for quality service even though it meant a higher expenditure per child.

Lesson Learned: Reduction in the number of clients to be served may need to be made in order to meet the qualitative goals of the program. Ideally, arrangements for possible changes should be negotiated with the funding sources before the program begins.

Conversely, sometimes changes are indicated that increase the number of clients served in a particular facet of the program and reallocation of resources needs to be made to meet the perceived need. The after-school class, originally planned for about fifteen older siblings, soon grew to some forty children that met twice a week. Shifts in the allocation of staff time were necessary to meet the increased size and complexity of the endeavor.

Lesson Learned: Sometimes program resources can be reallocated or supplemented to meet perceived needs. It may be practical to support these changes through collaboration with other organizations or through the use of volunteers, or both.

Issue No. 2: Early in the RFP *it became obvious that staff was experiencing severe limitations in their ability to communicate across linguistic and cultural boundaries.* There was a clear need for bilingual/bicultural staff. The award of Even Start funds in addition to the United Way funding in the fourth year of the program made it possible to add bilingual/ bicultural counselors. This opened up linguistic channels and enhanced communication informed by native perspectives. Improved communication enabled the staff to address complex family issues, to serve families in ways that could not have been realized previously, and to serve families who had hitherto been too difficult to include in the program because of the severity of their problems.

Lesson Learned: Staff who are linguistically and culturally, as well as psychologically capable of in-depth communication with families are indispensable in the program.

Issue No. 3: As the RFP *evolved it became increasingly evident that staff was not able to meet directly the full range of needs of the refugee families.* Prominent among family issues are domestic violence, substance abuse, addictive gambling, and psychosomatic illness, each of which is often a facet of post-traumatic stress disorder. The RFP gradually evolved referral relationships with specialized programs within and beyond the TIA/CC. These programs were helpful in several ways, but the fact is that there are very few people trained to treat these problems, especially when they are connected to the kinds of stressful histories that characterize the lives of so many of the refugees.

Lesson Learned: A deeper knowledge of the participants' needs during the proposal phase might have led to a more systematic provision for these needs in the program design. The most important lesson learned is that these problems are severely debilitating to individuals and their families and require in-depth, systematic treatment that is beyond the scope of the child-parent classes and the normal work of the Family Service component.

Issue No. 4: A key issue in a program such as this is how to strike a balance between embracing the cultural orientations of the client population on one hand, and emphasizing the cultural norms of the surrounding society on the other hand. This issue arises in at least two facets of the RFP. The first is in the context of the child-parent classes. Since the child-parent classes are designed to prepare the children for the school system they will be entering and to help the parents support their children in that system, the classes are based on the basic patterns of American schools. The parents bring traditional ideas about educational practice to the classes, stemming from childhood experience in their native cultures. The teachers introduce them to the educational methods that the children will encounter in public schools and try to teach them ways in which they can support the children in school. Chapter 3, for example, explains how the teachers model alternate ways of interacting with children that are more in line with present American culture.

The classes support the native cultures of the participants in ways that dovetail with the overall purpose. For example, parents are encouraged to tell their children stories and sing songs in their native language at home; the holidays of the participants are celebrated as part of the curriculum; and native words and phrases are included in the classes, especially in the context of learning the English counterparts. Most important, however, is the respect that teachers show through taking an interest in the families' cultures and taking an interest in each parent's situation and perspective. There is a basic respect shown in the act of situating the classes in people's homes. It says, among other things, that we understand that it is awkward and difficult for them to go long distances and enter strange environments.

Lesson Learned: The balance between placing emphasis on the cultural orientations of the client population and on the cultural norms of the surrounding society should be dictated by the pivotal goals of the program.

A second example of this issue is in the context of the Family Service component of the program. Some professionals question the RFP's strong emphasis on Western medicine, pointing out that not enough attention is given to traditional healing practices. The staff leans heavily toward Western medicine as the most effective choice, especially in the case of severe illness. It is the system of medicine that they know. In their view, there is a relatively poor quality of neighborhood medical services available to the families, including both Western medicine and traditional healing methods. Therefore, when Trudi and the bilingual counselors see medical problems that they deem to be serious, they are particularly active in getting the family to a medical clinic that Trudi and the counselors evaluate as high quality. Often families use both traditional healing methods and Western medicine. When they approach staff for medical help it is because they know that the staff have knowledge about treatment opportunities in the Western medical tradition.

Lesson Learned: Staff need to take the time and responsibility to sort through the options that might be available to clients and ultimately to operate from their best judgment in reaching a match between client and services.

Issue No. 5: Frequently, there is a significant lack of cultural understanding on the part of major service providers, such as hospitals and clinics, that interface with the refugee community.

Lesson Learned: In the design of future programs it would seem highly desirable to devote some portion of program resources to an ongoing orientation of service staff of key institutions to the habits, values, and perceptions of the refugee groups they serve. This kind of orientation, if done well, could in the long run diminish some of the need for program staff to intervene between these institutions and clients.

Issue No. 6: *Conflicts between the objectives of the program and the views of the families were evident throughout the six years.* An example of this conflict revolved around the parents' views of the staff and the time constraints inherent in the RFP. The parents saw the staff as helpful friends and expected their relationships with them to continue after the children were no longer in the classes. They relied on continuing service and could not understand why things should change when the classes ended. The RFP, the staff, and the services to the families were limited by the parameters of the program design. The staff tried their best to meet the needs of the families long after they had "left" the program, but this put considerable strain on their time and energies as they also had to work with newly recruited families.

Lesson Learned: This dilemma remains unsolved. It is most manifest in the families' continuing needs for medical help and for assistance to their teenage children long after their young children leave the preschool classes. The overall lesson is to periodically reformulate the program design and accompanying budget in relation to the main goal of serving families.

Part B: A Planning Outline

   I. Definition of the Problem: Questions to be Considered
      A. Who are the people to be served?
      B. What is their cultural background?
      C. What are their problems (from both the participants' and the service providers' perspectives)?
      D. What are the resources in the community that might benefit the people?
      E. What are the barriers to the clients receiving services?

   II. Goals
      A. Based on the definition of the problem, what should be the goals of the program?
      B. Are the goals supported by available resources?
      C. Are there some potential goals that are beyond

the resources of the program that could be accommodated by outside agencies? If so, should a referral process be built into the program?

III. Developmental Objectives
   A. What kinds of knowledge, skills, motivations, and self-confidence do children need to develop in order to reach the program goals?
      1. What methods would be used to assess children's abilities and difficulties (interviews with parents, public school teachers, observations, etc.)?
      2. How should an understanding of children's problems and strengths shape the program?
      3. Based on the goals of the program and the assessment of the children, what should be the major areas of focus in the children's program? Should the cognitive, language, motor, social-emotional areas be given equal weight, or should the emphasis be put on one or another of these domains?
      4. How should either the content or the process of the program change as children grow and develop?
   B. What circumstances need to be altered and capacities enhanced to provide a context for healthy child development?
      1. How will family needs be assessed? Interviews with adults and older children; observations of family interactions; assessment of living conditions; assessment of children; etc.?
      2. What is the availability of community resources that are amenable to working with refugee families?

IV. Process Objectives
   A. Based on the needs assessment, what kind of experiences will help parents develop the

knowledge, skills, perceptions, and self-confidence to provide a context for healthy child development?

1. How can parents learn and practice the skills and understanding necessary to support their children's learning prior to their entry into public school?
2. What do parents need to support their children's school work on an ongoing basis?
3. What is essential to their understanding of the school system, and how can this information be imparted most effectively?

B. How can the family component provide a temporary bridge between families and institutions?

1. How can the family service component strengthen a family's ability to deal effectively with institutions?
2. How can a program work with community agencies and institutions to make them more responsive to client families?

V. Resources

A. What resources are available through the agency or institution sponsoring the program, including personnel, space, and administrative support?

B. What community resources would be available to the program?

VI. Program Design

A. What should be the administrative structure of the program?

B. How should effective communication be ensured?

C. Given the goals, developmental objectives, process objectives, and likely resources, what should be the components of the program?

D. How should the program be staffed?

E. What should be the role of parents and community residents in the planning and implementation of the program?

VII. Recruitment and Training of Staff
  A. What qualities are required for each of the staff positions?
  B. What should be the preservice and in-service training plans?
  C. How should staff be supervised?

VIII. Volunteers
  A. Can volunteers play an effective role in this program design?
  B. If so, how will volunteers be recruited, trained, and supervised?

IX. Up-Front Planning
  A. After the general plan for the program is in place and the staff hired, what role will they play in the design of the specifics of the program?
  B. How much time should be devoted to this kind of detailed planning?
  C. Will potential participants play a role in the up-front planning process?

X. Recruitment of Participants
  A. What should be the criteria for accepting families into the program?
  B. What are likely to be the most successful avenues for recruiting families?
  C. What approach should be taken with agencies and individuals helpful in the recruitment effort?

XI. Evaluation
  A. Will there be an external evaluation, and if so, how can ongoing feedback to the staff be provided by the evaluators?

    B. If there is not an external evaluation, how can an ongoing internal assessment of the program provide productive insights for the staff?

    C. How can the practices and lessons learned by the program be documented for the benefit of other practitioners?

Appendixes

A Theoretical Framework for the Child-Parent Classes

In the Refugee Families Program, individual development is viewed as determined by biological factors that in turn are shaped by the culture in which the individual lives. Development continues throughout the life span but takes place most rapidly from the time of conception through infancy, childhood, and adolescence. Learning, in its broadest sense, is most easily acquired during this time when growth of the neurological system is most rapid. Children are taught what their culture determines they need to know. In Western societies a certain prescribed body of knowledge is taught in schools. In addition, children learn about their cultures indirectly through daily contact with the people in their lives and through interaction with the physical environment.

This general view of development is embedded in the theories of Jean Piaget, Lev S. Vygotsky, Erik H. Erikson, and Therese Benedek, among others.

Piaget's formulation of the development of cognition is rooted in his theory that children learn by interacting with their environments. As they take in new information from this interaction, they integrate it with what they already know. If this new knowledge does not fit with what is already known, the child has to change his view of the world. This process of reaching out to the environment and integrating the new information so that it fits existing ideas or changing those ideas to accommodate the new information plays a major role in the way children learn. This continuous back-and-forth process is the driving force for learning and cognitive development. Piaget's theory highlights the significance of allowing children to interact with their physical environments as an important means of learning.

Vygotsky offers another view of development that focuses on the social aspects of learning. Learning is seen as being mediated by adults and more competent children. As children mature they learn from their own interactions with the physical world, but that learning is imbedded in their cultures. What children learn and the way that they learn are determined by the society in which they live. This theory, which relies heavily on the cultural influences on development and learning, provides an important foundation for the Refugee Families Program.

The difference between Piaget and Vygotsky is clearly seen in the way each views the development of language. Piaget sees language as centered within the child and as developing from egocentric to social communication. Vygotsky views language as social in nature from the beginning, because language is by definition rooted in the culture.

Despite this difference in emphasis, both theories acknowledge the importance of play. Piaget describes play as the "ascendence of assimilation over accommodation," which means that when children play they emphasize the integrative part rather than the imitative aspect of learning. They can deal with new information and experiences on their own terms, and they can express their own feelings and ideas without being held to rigid notions of how things ought to be.

Vygotsky views play, which he defines as pretend play, as a means of encouraging the development of abstract thought and metacognition. As a child uses objects to represent things other than what they are and employs abbreviated actions to represent complex behaviors, the ability to use symbols is developed, and this in turn leads to abstract thought. Through pretend play children also become conscious of their behaviors and ideas because they have to think about what they are doing and how they are doing it. In play, their behavior is not automatic; it is calculated.

RFP concepts of emotional development are based in large part on Erikson's theories that specific personal and interpersonal issues come to the fore at each stage of an individual's life. There are eight stages in the life cycle. In infancy, psychological issues center on developing trust in others, which in turn leads to a trust in oneself. Toddlers are concerned with establishing their autonomy and their separateness from others, even those who love and care for them. Preschoolers focus on taking the initiative, of pushing out into the world and getting to know people outside of their families. For youngsters from six until early adolescence, school is the center of their lives. Gaining competence in their schoolwork through their own efforts wards off feelings of inferiority. Adolescence, young adulthood, adulthood, and old age complete the life cycle. Erikson refers to these stages of development as psychosocial, emphasizing the social or cultural, as well as the purely personal, aspects of an individual's experience. He notes that different cultures define the individual stages differently and put more or less emphasis upon them. This framework provides the foundation for understanding much of the children's behavior as they learn and interact with each other and with the adults in their society.

Erikson emphasizes that adults continue to change and develop. They do not remain stagnant. Their social and physical environments continue to have an important influence on them, and as these change, the lives of people change also. Parenthood requires caring for the next generation but the way it is defined by the culture provides the specifics of how it is to be carried out.

Therese Benedek's work on parenthood provides more concise ideas about the interactions of children and their parents and how parents and children influence each other. Since the parents' responses to the child are shaped in large part by their own experiences at that stage, it is common for parents to repeat with their children the kind of upbringing they themselves experienced. Positive experiences can be helpful when repeated in the new situation. On the other hand, painful or noxious experiences may interfere with parenting a child in positive ways.

Even though there is a tendency for parents to repeat behaviors learned early in life, for many it is a time to redo old patterns and heal old wounds as they nurture their own children. Parents are most successful at making these changes in learned patterns of behavior when they have the support of people they feel they can lean on and trust.

The parents in the Refugee Families Program need to

acquire new information about how and what children are expected to learn in this culture and about the education the children will receive. Parents also need help in developing new skills to better cope with their new circumstances. Sending children to school regularly and seeing that they are properly dressed for the weather are examples of how many parents need to change old habits. Other school requirements, such as making sure the children have prescribed inoculations, must also be learned. For those brought up in rural environments, learning about urban life is particularly important and often difficult.

The RFP relies in part on adult education methods to develop the content and strategies for working effectively with the parents, keeping in mind the cultural differences between the participants and the staff. In addition to the cultural difference, class differences are taken into account. Two people from the same country may differ markedly in their ideas and values if they are from different classes.

Contemporary adult education is based on the concept that the teacher facilitates learning rather than transmitting information. Current ideas about early education that give children a great deal of control over their education are not so different from this approach to adult education. In both situations choices are provided, and the learners are encouraged to take responsibility for their own learning. However, in both instances the teacher needs to transmit a certain amount of information, in addition to helping the students make use of what they already know. Although these ideas are given credence in the Refugee Families Program, they are tempered with the need to be culturally sensitive to the expectations of the participants.

Parent education requires dealing with information and ideas that have great emotional impact. The way parents were raised is deeply ingrained in their psychological makeup, and change often implies relinquishing the ideas of their parents and renouncing their original culture. Helping parents change while still retaining their sense of self and their cultural bonds becomes a real challenge. When the country of origin of newcomers is very different from their new country, there are added difficulties.

All interactions with parents and children require special

sensitivity on the part of the staff to cultural and class differences. The more obvious differences (such as protocols for eye contact, physical touching, greetings, and entering homes) are comparatively easy to learn. It is the more subtle issues that can be misunderstood and misconstrued. The tone of one's voice or body language can relay messages or change the meaning of words. It is important therefore to be alert to all aspects of cultural differences, while building positive and reliable relationships. When people like and trust each other some of the abrasions that can accompany cross-cultural transactions are forgiven.

APPENDIX

B Curriculum for the Child-Parent Classes

When TIA/CC first initiated the Refugee Families Program (RFP), several curricula were examined for the child-parent classes. However, because of the unique design of the RFP, existing curricula for preschools were not adequate to meet the needs of the population served and to further the goals of the program. It was therefore necessary to design a curriculum specifically for this program. The curriculum that was finally developed adapted ideas and strategies from several other curricula and combined them in ways that were consistent with the particular requirements of the RFP. Before describing the curriculum used in the child-parent classes, it is appropriate to discuss the process that can be used by others in designing a curriculum.

Population Served

The most important factor to be considered in designing a curriculum is the population it will serve. The families in the RFP represent several different language and cultural groups (see chapter 1), mostly Cambodians and Vietnamese, but also Laotians, Ethiopians, Somalis, and Afghans. Although these families come from diverse cultures, they share the critical characteristics of refugee status.

Most of the individuals are not proficient in English, and many do not speak the language at all. A large number have received little or no education and do not read or write in any language. Most, but not all, of the refugees come from rural backgrounds and have difficulty adjusting to urban life. In addition, they live in poor neighborhoods, besieged by crime, drug trafficking, and gang violence. Many of the participants in our program have been traumatized by war, by the loss of family members, by the separation of children from parents, and by the hardships of refugee camps. As a result, they often suffer from psychological and social problems and easily fall victim to alcohol, drug, and gambling addictions. All the families face the difficulty of adjusting to a new culture and environment, and these stresses have resulted in some dysfunctional families. Inevitably, almost all the families in the Refugee Families Program have trouble supporting their children's school life and making use of the community resources available to them.

Structure of the Program

Another important consideration in developing a curriculum is the structure of the program in which it is embedded. The classes of the Refugee Families Program are designed to accommodate small groups of parents and children who meet in the apartment of one of the participants. This format allows teachers to give individual attention to those who need it and provides an environment that is familiar to both the children and the adults. Although the variety of materials and activities is more limited than what is usually found in preschool classrooms, the small classes promote closeness among the children and among the adults and encourage learning from one another. For example, if one parent knows more English, she can act as an interpreter for the others and teach them some vocabulary. For those who live isolated lives, the small groups are a means of promoting connectedness among the individuals or families.

Participation in the classes helps the children begin to acquire the skills necessary for public school. Even though the classes in the RFP are small, they offer a semblance of the group life the children will experience in school. The classes offer an opportunity for children to improve the skills that will be required, and the parents benefit from watching the teacher demonstrate school expectations.

Cultural Differences in Education and Child Rearing

A third issue influencing the curriculum design is the varying approaches to child rearing and views of education that families bring with them. The families participating in the RFP are not familiar with the ideas espoused by contemporary early education professionals in this country and taught in teacher education schools. Current theories that emphasize interaction between the child and his or her environment place the locus of control with the child rather than with the teacher. This kind of relationship between students and teachers is antithetical to many non-Western cultures.

The views of the RFP families tend to be based on notions of schoolrooms where the teacher transmits information to the students in a didactic fashion. The children are expected to memorize the information and learn skills by copying the movements of the teacher. Parents' roles are not to teach school subjects to the children or even help them with their homework, but rather to teach manners and self-help skills, leaving the instruction of reading and writing to the teacher.

Children and Parents Together

Another determinant of the RFP curriculum is the goal of reaching both children and parents during the classes. Efforts are made to meet the educational needs of the children so that they are better prepared for entrance into school. At the same time, parents are helped to support their children in school, which often requires changing their views of how they relate to the school and the teachers, as well as their own children.

Schedule

The schedule of the classes also makes special demands on the curriculum. Each class meets twice a week rather than every day. Therefore, special attention has to be paid to providing continuity to the topics.

Implementation

Implementation of the RFP curriculum borrows from two techniques used in many home-visiting projects. Although the RFP is not a home-visiting program, it shares some elements of such an approach. Both children and parents are included in the instruction, which takes place in the participant's home. In one home-visiting approach, the teacher works directly with the children, while the parent observes the methods used and tries to imitate them with her child. In the other approach, the home visitor works directly with the parent, teaching her how to teach her child.

An adaptation of both these techniques is used in implementing the RFP curriculum. The teachers work directly with the children. They teach them skills, provide appropriate games and materials, read stories, sing songs, and perform all the roles and duties of a preschool teacher. In addition, they help the parents participate appropriately in the children's activities. The teachers guide the parents in supporting the children's learning without taking over from them, and soon the parents begin to understand the new educational methods and feel comfortable helping their preschool children in the class activities. Parents and children are given activities to do together at home, which also helps the parents feel more comfortable about these tasks and prepares them for continued support as the children progress through public school.

English is used in the classes, but parents are encouraged to use their native language at home to tell their children stories and to discuss what they did in class. The use of the home language perpetuates and shows respect for the culture of the families and provides opportunities for children to learn concepts in the language with which they are most familiar.

Practice Principles

The work with both the children and the parents is guided by principles originating from the theories discussed in appendix A, with careful consideration given to the cultural backgrounds of the participants.

Children

1. Activities and interactions are individualized so that the learning styles and needs of the children are taken into account.
2. Both implicit (play, art, games, etc.) and explicit (songs, finger plays, reading stories, etc.) techniques are used to teach the children and improve their English vocabulary.
3. Teachers show respect for the language and culture of the children by including songs, games, stories, and crafts of

the children's cultures in the group activities. Celebration of important holidays of their native countries is also a part of the curriculum.

4. Children learn the rules of the "school game" during class.
5. Efforts are made to build in as many successful experiences as possible for the children through providing appropriate activities.
6. Children are aided in feeling comfortable and in control by a consistent schedule and consistent expectations.
7. Children are given the opportunities to choose their own activities in order to foster autonomy and to emphasize successful completion of tasks.
8. Play is included in each class to further intellectual development and to encourage creativity.

Adults

1. Teachers model adult-child interaction for parents based on school expectations. They help parents understand the increasing capabilities of young children.
2. Teachers model the expected teacher-parent relationship and also make it explicit.
3. Parents are encouraged to take part in group activities, and to help their children in appropriate ways.
4. Suggestions are made about the role of the parents in working with their children on homework assignments.
5. Teachers help parents use community resources by taking children and parents on trips to libraries, museums, zoos, and so on.

Philosophy and Objectives of Developmental Areas

Cognitive Development

Children learn by doing. They learn through their interaction with materials and people. We provide children with many opportunities to play with objects, to use symbols, and to practice many cognitive skills. We also ask questions and encourage exploration and experimentation. Through this process, children generate new ideas and gain an understanding of their world.

The objectives are as follows: to develop a positive attitude toward learning, to expand critical thinking skills, to cultivate creative problem solving abilities, to progress through content areas that are compatible with ability and developmental level, and to acquire information that will lead to a better understanding of the world.

Language Development

While growth in language skills is part of the cognitive developmental process, it is important for us to put an emphasis on this developmental area because the children in our classes are just beginning to learn English as their second language. The exposure to English happens formally as we present particular vocabulary during the teacher-led activity, music, or book time; and it happens informally as we discuss the children's activities during free play or art. Language acquisition occurs in one-to-one interactions, as well as in small groups.

Although we teach English, we encourage parents to use their own language with their children. We believe that a strong base in the children's first language will facilitate their learning of another language and will support family cohesiveness and cultural identity.

The objectives are as follows: to expand verbal communication skills in both first and second languages, to improve listening skills in both first and second languages, and to attain a foundation for written communication skills.

Social/Emotional Growth

Preschool children are learning to be independent and to take control of themselves. They are also learning how to interact and to express themselves in socially acceptable ways. We strive to provide an environment that promotes these qualities by helping children to feel safe and accepted by the teachers. We show that we value the children's creativity and their efforts to try new activities by listening and responding positively to them. We stress the importance of this type of interaction to the parents and encourage them and the other children in the group to do the same.

The objectives are as follows: to develop a positive self-concept, to begin to act in cooperative and pro-social ways, to take an interest in learning new activities, to increase the capacity to concentrate on tasks, and to express feelings in appropriate and effective ways.

Physical Development

Preschool-aged children are constantly in the process of refining their motor skills. Our classes provide activities and materials, at varying levels, with which children can develop gross and fine motor skills. New challenges are introduced as children become ready for them. The teachers offer guidance and encouragement and work with parents to interact in a similar manner with their children.

The objectives are as follows: to gain awareness of the senses, to improve gross motor skills, to increase fine motor skills, and to develop mental and physical coordination.

Parental Involvement in the Preschool Program

The active participation of parents in the home-based classes is an integral part of the program. The parents are encouraged to work with their children and learn to help them in ways that will support their development. The teachers provide models for the parents to interact with their children, emphasizing support of the children's efforts without the parents doing too much for them. Parents are also encouraged to use praise and other methods of positive reinforcement as they practice helping their children in a school setting.

Just as the children learn by doing, so do the parents benefit from a dynamic approach to instruction. They learn about the school system their children will enter and the method of teaching that is new to them. Not only do the parents learn from the involvement in the class activities, but they enjoy doing things with their hands and having opportunities to be creative with some of the art activities and constructive materials.

The teachers guide the parents in learning new methods of working with their children based upon the following concepts:

- Children learn through play
- Children learn better when the process is pleasurable
- The environment provides learning opportunities
- Learning can be exploratory and process-oriented rather than product-oriented

- Affirmation is important in the learning process and can strengthen a child's motivation
- Interacting with and observing the development of one's own child is enjoyable and rewarding

Preschool Class Units

Classes are organized around thematic units but focus on particular concepts and basic skills. All areas of development are taken into account in planning the activities and materials for the classes, and careful consideration is given to the ages and stages of the children. Some classes have children of approximately the same ages, while others have a wider age range among the children, so lesson plans have to be tailored to each group. The time devoted to each of the units varies depending upon the ages and developmental levels of the children.

Each thematic unit described below lists appropriate toys, activities, and books. These are mentioned only once, although they may be used in several different units. In addition to the books listed, teachers use books borrowed from the local libraries. Additional arts, crafts, and seasonal activities often augment the units. Some of these ideas are listed below.

Getting Started with Colors (Two–three weeks)
We begin with colors because children often distinguish objects first by their color. The activities familiarize the children and parents with the concept of classification, and the simplicity of color vocabulary immediately engages both parents and children whose command of the English language is minimal. During these first weeks, the participants are able to become familiar with one another and with the routine and structure of the class.

The objectives are as follows: to acquaint each child with the routine and with one another, to enable the child to distinguish the primary and secondary colors, and to familiarize the child with the names of these colors.

- *Free play:*

Soft blocks	Bristle blocks
Duplos	Petal play
Simple Lauri puzzles	Lots-o-links

- *Teacher-led activities:*

Hand out crayons	Sort colors
Fish pond	Unifix cubes
Matching	Color flashcards
Rainbow colors	Gumball game
Color clowns	Unifix bingo
Paint cans	Wiggles game
Color dice	Candyland bingo
Candyland	Cellophane plates
Colors around the room	Color dog bone game

- *Books:*
  Is It Red? Is It Yellow? Is It Blue? (Hoban)
  Colors (Reiss)
  The Color of Things (Hoban)
  Planting a Rainbow (Ehlert)
  White Rabbit's Color Book (Baker)
  Red, Blue, Yellow Shoe (Hoban)
  My First Look At Colors (Random House)
  Colors (Lynn)
  What Color? (Pragoff)
  Mouse Paint (Walsh)
  The Brambleberry's Animal Book of Colors (Mayer/McDermott)
  Color (Rossetti/Teichman)
  Who Said Red? (Serfozo)
  Colors (Jeuness/de Bourgoing)
  Brown Bear, Brown Bear, What Do You See? (Martin, Jr./Carle)

- *Arts and crafts:*
  Free coloring
  Color classification collage
  Water coloring
  Colorstrip cans

- *Movement and music:*
  "Hello" and "Good-bye" songs
  Go around the room and point to the colors
  "Color Song"

Shapes (Three–four weeks)

Because we live in a multidimensional world, shapes are an integral part of the early math curriculum. Children benefit from the opportunity to work with various shapes. They can experiment with the shapes to see what can be done with them and how they relate to each other. Like colors, shapes provide a simple way for children to begin to categorize objects, and to expand their vocabularies.

The objectives are as follows: to provide a variety of hands-on experiences with shapes, to encourage the child to recognize and name shapes in the immediate environment, and to encourage the child to use shapes in creative ways.

- *Free play:*

  Lace-ups
  Pattern blocks
  Shape matching board
  Shapes and colors
  Colorama
  Shape of things
  Playskills kit

  Shape sorter
  Peg Pen
  Magnadoodle
  Giroform puzzles
  Magnatooli
  Magnetic wooden shapes

- *Teacher-led activities:*

  Shape boxes
  Matching
  Flashcards
  Shape dominoes
  Shape dice

  Shape sorting
  Feltboard shapes
  Shape lotto
  Dino-bingo
  Shapes in the room

- *Books:*

  My First Look at Shapes (Random House)
  Circles, Triangles, and Squares (Hoban)
  Shapes (Reiss)
  Shapes, Shapes, Shapes (Hoban)
  Shapes (Knightley)
  City Shapes (Baum)
  Shapes and Things (Hoban)

- *Arts and crafts:*

  Shape collage
  Shape costumes
  Shape sponge painting
  Shape stamps
  Shape classification collage
  Cardboard roll printing

  Shape stencils
  Playdough shapes
  Popsicle collage
  Jell-o shapes
  Shape printing
  Triangle texture collage

- *Movement and music:*
  "Shape song"
  Shape hunt
  Shape costume activities
  Beanbag shape toss
  Walk to the shape

Size (Two–three weeks)
  The unit on shapes naturally flows into a focus on size. The children use shapes as tools in beginning to learn about size. They are introduced to beginning ideas about measurement and to basic concepts such as comparisons and sequencing.
  The objectives are as follows: to provide the child with opportunities to manipulate shapes and objects representing a wide variety of sizes, to introduce the child to size vocabulary, and to introduce the concept of opposites.

- *Free play:*

Size sorter	Chalkboards
Attribute blocks	Sequence cards
Stacking cups	Stacking boxes

- *Teacher-led activities:*

Feltboard activities	Sorting attribute blocks
Big/small grab bag	Big/small sorting
Matching activities	Measuring children

- *Books:*
  Big Fish, Little Fish (Asch)
  Sizes (Pienkowski)
  Is It Larger? Is It Smaller? (Hoban)
  My First Look at Sizes (Random House)
  Big Ones, Little Ones (Hoban)
  Angus Thought He Was Big (Graham/Wood)

- *Arts and crafts:*

Size sponge painting	Playdough shape sizes
Size classification collage	Big/small stencils
Multitextured shape collage	

- *Movement and music:*
  "I Am Very, Very Big . . ."
  Big/small body movements
  Walk to big/small shapes

Patterns (Two weeks)
Learning about patterns reviews and reinforces the children's understanding of shapes, sizes, and colors. It also increases vocabulary and builds a foundation for mathematical concepts.

The objectives are as follows: to furnish the children with a broad range of activities in which they can experience patterns in visual, auditory, and physical ways, to review material from the previous units, to introduce the relationship between patterns and order, to increase the children's awareness of patterns in the environment, and to encourage them to create their own patterns.

- *Free play:*

Wooden beads	Unifix cubes
Sequencers	Beads and baubles
Magnet board shapes	Lots-o-links
Lauri stack-up people	Toweriffics

- *Teacher-led activities:*

Feltboard activities	Unifix cube activities
Making fruit kabobs	Color strip activities
Pretzel stick/cheese patterns	

- *Books:*
  Shape Space (Falwell)
  Dots, Spots, Speckles, and Stripes (Hoban)

- *Arts and crafts:*
  Bead necklaces
  Pattern collages
  Paper chains

- *Movement and music:*
  Pattern clapping
  Rhythm instrument patterns
  Movement/patterns

Animals (Four–five weeks)
Children's natural interest in animals facilitates further language development. They acquire new vocabulary as they learn animal names, and they use it to talk about the animals and to impersonate them. This development continues as they classify the animals according to where they live and what they eat, etc.

The objectives are as follows: to familiarize the child with names of common wild and domestic animals, to enhance language development through the use of classification, to encourage dramatic play, and to cultivate an appreciation of the natural world.

- *Free play:*
  Large model animals
  Dinosaurs
  Lauriland farmyard
  Plastic animal puzzle/
  stencils
  Playskills kit
  Animal stick-ons
  Playdough

  Tub-o-animals
  Barn/animals
  Lace-ups
  Animal dominoes
  Wood animals
  Animal lotto

- *Teacher-led activities:*
  Animal dominoes
  Match-n-spell
  Crazy mixed-up animals
  Feltboard animals
  Barnyard scene
  Photo matching
  Animal lotto
  Animal parts
  Zoo field trip

  Animal memory
  Velcro animals
  Animal sorting
  Jungle animal zoo
  Animal photos
  Farm animal bingo
  Animal homes
  Animal videos
  Jungle puzzle

- *Books:*
  Animal Go Round (Morris)
  Amazing Animals (Ward)
  Chickens Aren't the Only Ones (Heller)
  Animals Should Definitely Not Act Like People (Barret)
  Who Lives Here (Snow)
  What Color? (Pragoff)
  Stuck in the Mud (Croser/Vassiliou)

The Mitten (Brett)
Farmer in the Dell (Rae)
Farm Babies (Rice/Ogden)
Animal Babies (McNaught)
Is Your Mama a Llama? (Guarino/Kellog)
Look (Wilson)
Who Said Meow? (Polushkin/Weiss)
This is the Farmer (Tafuri)
Babies' Book of Animals (Priddy)
Have You Seen My Duckling? (Tafuri)
Early Morning in the Barn (Tafuri)
Animals Born Alive and Well (Heller)
Seasons on the Farm (Miller)
Aardvarks Disembark (Jones)
Wild Animals (Snapshot)
Farm Noises (Miller)
Old McDonald (Rounds)
Brown Bear (Martin/Carle)
Children's Zoo (Hoban)
Animals, Animals (Carle)
Zoo 1,2,3 (Carle)
Big Ones, Little Ones (Hoban)
Hoot, Howl, Hiss
Feed the Animals (Rey)
Very Hungry Caterpillar (Carle)
Animals, A-Z (Johnson)
Farm Alphabet Book (Miller)
Very Busy Spider (Carle)
Grouchy Ladybug (Carle)
Watch Where You Go (Noll)
Big Al (Yoshi)
Jiggle, Wiggle, Prance
Orchestranimals (Kamper)
Baby Animals (Kaufman)
Where's My Baby (Ray)
Who Says Moo? (Kalish)
Animals (Greeley)

- *Art:*
  Cotton ball sheep   Paper plate pigs
  Paper plate lions   Farm scene

Stuffed farm animals

Animal printing with
cookie cutters

Make animals with
Playdough

Jungle scene

Butterfly prints

Animal puppets

Animal sponge painting

Coffee filter butterfly

- *Movement and music:*
  Animal puppets
  Brown bear puppets
  Tape-recorded animal sounds
  "Mary Had a Little Lamb"
  Exercise with *Jiggle, Wiggle, Prance*
  Animal masks
  Animal charades
  "Old Grey Cat"

Numbers (Four–six weeks)

This unit builds upon what the child already intuitively grasps about mathematical concepts and numbers. We engage the children in enjoyable activities in which they experiment with quantity, shape, and size of manipulating objects. The children are exposed to written numbers through books, but no emphasis is put on learning to write numbers.

The objectives are as follows: to furnish the children with objects they can manipulate by matching, measuring, etc., to provide opportunities to experience quantities visually and physically, to assist the child in acquiring language to talk about quantities, and to increase the child's awareness of quantities in the environment.

- *Free play:*
  Tinkertoys
  Unifix cubes
  Train number puzzle

  Dominoes
  Wooden number puzzles
  Playskills kit

- *Teacher-led activities:*
  Hi-Ho Cherry-o
  Sorting
  Number buckets
  Number bingo
  Egg carton number games
  Number dice

  Flash cards
  Fish pond with numbers
  Number memory
  Egg carton
  Shaker number game
  Matching

Feltboard counting   Unifix cubes
Watermelon slices   Bean counting cards
Pick and hold   Clothes hanger counters

- *Books:*
  26 Letters and $.99 (Hoban)
  Who's Counting (Tafuri)
  Brambleberry's Animal Book of Counting (Mayer/ McDermott)
  Anno's Book of Counting (Anno)
  Ten Black Dots (Crews)
  Ten Little Ducks (Hammond)
  10, 9, 8 (Bang)
  The Icky Bug Counting Book (Pallotta/Masiello)
  The Right Number of Animals
  I Can Count (Simon & Schuster)
  Ten Big Babies (Priest/Helmer)
  My First Look at Numbers (Random House)
  1, 2, 3 (Sara Lynn)
  The Very Hungry Caterpillar (Carle)
  1, 2, 3 to the Zoo (Carle)
  My First 1, 2, 3 Book (Conran)
  Lifesize Animal Counting Book (Dorling Kindersley)
  Can You Imagine? (Gardner)
  Fish Eyes (Ehlert)
  Paddington 123 (Bond)
  Count and See (Hoban)
  Numbers (Anderson)
  Five Little Monkeys (Christelow)
  More Than One (Hoban)
  One Good Horse (Scott)
  1, 2, 3 (Seiden)
  One Pair, Two Pair (McMillan)
  How Many? (Pragoff)

- *Arts and crafts:*
  Counting caterpillars   Lace-up numbers
  Texture book   Glue on 1–10
  Ice cream cones   Sponge painting with
  Number cans   numbers
  "Free-lance" painting

- *Movement and music:*
  "Ten Little Fingers"   Number footsteps
  "Six Little Ducks"   Clap and count
  "Alligator Song"   "Frog song"
  Counting with exercise   Clothespin drop

My Body (Three–four weeks)
The body is a marvelous creation. It is important that the children become comfortable with the uniqueness of their own bodies and develop an awareness of the many things they can do with them. It is also important that the children learn to respect their bodies and those of other children in the class.

The objectives are as follows: to increase children's awareness of their bodies and their uniqueness; to provide an atmosphere in which the children can explore the many ways of using their bodies; to promote a positive self-concept; and to familiarize them with the words for body parts and movements.

- *Free play:*
  Dolls   Lauriland
  Wooden face puzzle   Plastic people
  Play people   Petal play
  Magnetic blocks   Playdough
  Wooden face puzzle

- *Teacher-led activities:*
  Identify facial/body parts on own body
  "What can you do with your _____?"
  Face puzzle
  Feltboard face and body parts
  "Point to your partner's _____"
  Flashcards
  Cut-and-paste body parts
  Measuring children

- *Books:*
  Tail, Toes, Eyes, Ears, Nose (Burton)
  Clap Your Hands (Cauley)
  Here Are My Hands (Archambault/Frand)
  My Feet Do (Holzenthen)

- *Arts and crafts:*

Footprints/paint	Body tracing
Spackle hand prints	Face drawing
Puppets of self	Self-portraits

- *Movement and music:*

"Look and Do" flash cards	"Clap Your Hands"
"Head, Shoulders, Knees, and Toes"	"Me"
	Hap Palmer cassette
	Hokey-Pokey
"Old MacDonald Had a Body"	Copy me (Simon says)

Clothing (Two–three weeks)

The clothing unit provides an opportunity to review body parts and promotes the importance of the use of seasonally appropriate attire. The availability of a variety of clothing in the apartment where class is held facilitates this process.

The objectives are as follows: to familiarize children with common clothing vocabulary, to acquaint them with clothing that is appropriate for each season, and to increase the awareness of similarities and differences among children's clothing.

- *Free play:*

Dolls and accessories	Snap-on blocks
Lace-ups	Contrast puzzles

- *Teacher-led activities:*
  Feltboard dress-up dolls
  "What would you wear if it's _____"
  Clothing review with magazine photographs
  "What are you wearing?"

- *Books:*
  Where Do I Put My Clothes? (Bonkar)
  One Wet Jacket (Tafuri)
  Caps, Hats, Socks, Mittens (Hoban)
  Hats, Hats, Hats (Morris)

- *Arts and crafts:*
  Glue-on clothing
  Hot/cold collage
  Felt doll designs

- *Movement and music:*
  Exercise with Ernie
  Look and do-exercise

The Senses (Two–three weeks)
This unit continues to reinforce the functions of the body and the vocabulary appropriate for the subject. The senses and their uses are emphasized and the children's sensitivity to the ways in which their senses function separately and together is heightened.

The objectives are as follows: to furnish the child with a variety of sensory experiences, to encourage the child's intuitive awareness of opposites, and to enhance the child's personal awareness by discussing personal preferences of taste, smell, sight, touch, and hearing.

- *Free play:*
  Imagination builders
  Building logs

- *Teacher-led activities:*
  Hearing: "What's that sound?", Recording and playing it back
  Sight: "What can you see?"
  Touch: Feely bag, texture box
  Smell: "What's that smell?"
  Taste: Taste test

- *Books:*
  My Five Senses (Aliko)
  The Ear Book (Le Sieg/McKoe)
  The Eye Book (Perkins/O'Brien)
  Look Again (Hoban)
  Take Another Look (Hoban)

- *Arts and crafts:*
  Finger painting   Egg dyeing
  Popcorn making   Clay play

- *Movement and music:*
  Rhythm instruments
  Make recordings of voices and instruments
  "This Is What I Can Do"

Emotions (One–two weeks)

Emotional growth is a key area of development. Children need to be able to express their emotions and have appropriate means with which to express them. It is also important that they begin to understand how to identify and respect the feelings of other people as well.

The objectives are as follows: to provide an environment in which feelings are validated, to promote early conflict resolution, to cultivate self-awareness, and to encourage dramatic play.

- *Free play:*
  Dolls   Play house
  Toy animals   Blocks

- *Teacher-led activities:*
  Emotions flash cards
  Guess the (teacher's) face
  "What makes you feel _____?"
  "Take turns making faces"
  Matching
  Emotion puzzle
  Emotion spinner

- *Books:*
  Alexander and the Terrible . . . Day (Viorst)
  I Was So Mad (Mayer)
  Where the Wild Things Are (Sendak)
  Feelings (Aliki)
  Feelings Alphabet (Lalli)
  I'm Not Tired (O'Brian)
  The Pain and the Great One (Blume)

- *Arts and crafts:*
  Happy/sad mask
  Free-form emotions collage
  Emotions classification collage

- *Movement and music:*
  "Now I'm Very _____"
  "If You're Happy . . ."

The Alphabet (Four–five weeks)

Introducing the alphabet is important for school readiness. While it is not necessary for the children to learn all of the letters at this time, it is helpful for them to realize that these symbols have meaning.

The objectives are as follows: to provide the children with a chance to physically manipulate letters; to familiarize them with letters and their sounds, when appropriate; to encourage the children to notice letters in their surroundings; and to assist the children who are ready to begin to recognize and write their names.

- *Free play:*

Hi-Ho alphabet game	Alphabet blocks
ABC puzzles	Small wood blocks
Magnet board	Alphabet avalanche
Alpha sewing cards	Slates and chalk
Magnadoodle	Match n' spell
Alphabet train	Stickees

- *Teacher-led activities:*

Alphabet flashcards	Sorting letters
Matching with feltboard letters	Magnetic board letters
	Letter concentration
Name cups	Alphabet lotto
Find letters in the feely bag	Alphabet soup
	Body boggle
Puppet/bone game with letters	Name cards

- *Books:*
  Farm Alphabet Book (Miller)
  Homemade Alphabet Book (Amaral)
  A is For Angry (Boynom)
  A, B, See (Hoban)
  Eating the Alphabet (Ehlert)
  Demi's Find the Animals ABC (Demi)
  The Most Amazing Hide-and-Seek-Alphabet Book (Crowther)
  ABC (Knightley)
  26 Letters and $0.99 (Hoban)
  A to Z: Look and See (Johnson)
  My First ABC Book (Conran)
  Alphabears (Hague/Hague)
  Animals A to Z (McPhail)
  Feelings Alphabet (Lalli)

- *Arts and crafts:*
  Cut-out Playdough letters
  Sponge painting with letters
  Letter stamps

- *Movement and music:*
  "The Alphabet Song"

All About Me (Three–four weeks)
   By this time, the children will have developed some vocabulary to talk about themselves and their surroundings. They can use words that they have learned throughout the year to describe themselves. They also have the opportunity to talk about their families and their homes.
   The objectives are as follows: to increase the children's awareness of their abilities, to celebrate the individuality of each child, to encourage the children to use new vocabulary to describe their families and immediate surroundings, and to provide a sense of closure to the classes.

- *Free play:*
  Play house
  Wooden community
  puzzle

  Adventure floor puzzle
  Town floor mat
  Marble run

- *Teacher-led activities:*
  Measure the children
  Home environment flash
   cards
  Make "About Me" books
  (Over several sessions)
  Home tour

  Home environment
  stickees
  Hand out photos from
  year
  Pass out certificates

- *Books:*
  Play Day (Scarry)
  All About You (Anholt)
  We Are All Alike, We Are All Different (Cheltenham
  Kindergarten)
  A House is a House for Me (Hoberman/Fraser)
  We Are Children (Amaral)
  Who Uses This (Miller)
  Bathtime (Roffey)
  Going to the Dentist (Rogers)

The Wheels on the Bus (Ziefert/Barufi)
My First Book of Words (Shiffman)
Listen To The City (Pellegrino/Wong)
Early Words (Scarry)
Is This You? (DelVecchio/Maestro)

- *Arts and crafts:*

  Self-portraits   Portrait of family
  Home classification   Portrait of home
  collage   Make cover for book

- *Movement and song:*
  "The Wheels on the Bus"
  "This Is What I Can Do"
  "This is the Way"
  Exercise with *Blue Bug*

Seasonal Activities

Autumn activities include:

- Nature walk
- Tempera leaf printing
- Crayon leaf rubbings
- Pumpkin seed roasting
- Moon festival activities (moon cakes, lanterns)
- Leaf collecting
- Leaf stenciling
- Pumpkin carving
- "Fall Song"

Books used:

- *Autumn* (McNaughton)
- *What Happens In Autumn* (Venino)
- *Autumn* (Thomas/Millard)
- *Look, Look, Look* (Hoban)
- *The Biggest Pumpkin Ever* (Kroll)
- *Picking Apples and Pumpkins* (Hutchings/Hutchings)
- *Red Leaf, Yellow Leaf* (Ehlert)

Winter activities include:

- Discussing winter clothing
- Snow painting

- Creating a winter scene
- Celebration of Vietnamese New Year (zodiac/animals, Lucky Game, flowers, party)
- Snow play
- Ice cube painting

Books used:

- *The Snowy Day* (Keats)
- *Geraldine's Big Snow* (Keller)
- *Snow Day* (Maestro)
- *Celebrating New Year* (Yuan-Shian)
- *Lion Dancer* (Watts/Slovey-Low)
- *Tet: The New Year* (Tran/Vo-Dinh)
- *Why Rat Comes First* (Yen/Yoshida)

Spring activities include:

- Nature walk
- Plant bean seeds and chart growth
- Cambodian New Year (zodiac, animal mask, Cambodian songs (Lucky Game, party)

Books used:

- *The Carrot Seed* (Krauss/Johnson)
- *Growing Vegetable Soup* (Ehlert)
- *The Tiny Seed* (Carle)
- *The Tree* (Jeunesse/DeBourgoing/Broutin)
- *Planting a Rainbow* (Ehlert)
- *Dara's Cambodian Year* (Chiemroum/Pin)

Summer activities include:

- Visit parks to use playground equipment and play outdoor games
- Visit beach for sand and water play
- Other suggested field trips: Aquarium/Oceanarium, Children's Museum, North Park Nature Center, Botanic Gardens, Museum of Natural History

Books used:

- *What Will the Weather Be Like Today?* (Rogers/Kazuko)
- *Weather* (Jeunesse/de Bourgoing/Kiffke)

Additional Art Activities

Additional art activities included the following:

- Open art with the following media

Water color	Tempera
Crayons	Colored pencils
Water color crayons	Water color pencils
Oil pastels	Finger paints
Chalk pastels	Markers
Playdough	Clay
Collage materials	

- Applying paint with the following materials

Daubers	Droppers
Spray bottles	Roll-on bottles
Marbles	String
Combs	Ice cubes
Straws	Screens
Cookie cutters	Brushes (includes splat-
Various shapes	tering)
Styrofoam	

- Crafts
  Coffee filter flowers
  Plaster of paris prints
  Eye-dropper, coffee filter butterflies
  Stained glass windows
  Paper weaving

C Program Forms

Weekly Lesson Plan

Dates: _____

Theme: _____

Class Numbers _____ & _____

Group Number _____

Day	Free Play		Teacher-led Activity	Snack	Book Time	Movement & Music	Arts & Crafts		Homework
		Opening Time						Closing Time	
		Opening Time						Closing Time	

Client Intake

Date_____

Child_____   Ethnicity_____

Address and Phone_____

Household Members
            Name   Birthdate   Relationship   School

1. ....

2. ....

3. ....

4. ....

5. ....

6. ....

7. ....

Date of Arrival_____   Sponsor Agency_____

IDPA Case No._____   Agency No._____

Family members working (who? where? when? what?)

_____

Other relatives (who? where? address in Chicago?)

_____

_____

Current health status _____

_____

Family goes to Wilson Clinic? (translator's name) _____

Dr. _____ Dr. _____ Dr. _____

Other doctors/clinics _____

Family history (background, escape, refugee camp experience, education, health, etc.):

_____

_____

_____

_____

_____

_____

Community support

- MAA (staff person? frequency?)

_____

- Temple/Church (where? frequency?)

_____

- Other

_____

_____

Additional comments

_____

_____

_____

_____

What do parents hope to get from their participation in the Refugee Families Program?

_____

_____

Class Report

Group No. _____ Day _____ Date _____ Teacher _____

Attendance: (children) _____ (adults) _____

Sequence of class/activities:

Parenting issues discussed:

Comments (class process, areas for improvement, observations, etc.):

Group Participant List

Class days and time _____

Group No. _____ Beginning date _____

Teacher _____

Family name _____ Ethnicity _____

Address and phone _____

Child	Age	Caregiver	Relation	Address/Phone
1.				
2.				
3.				
4.				
5.				

Child Profile Chart

Child's Name and Ethnicity	Date of birth	Cycle/group number	Early termination	Completion of cycle	Successive cycle once weekly	Successive cycle twice weekly	Pre-K application	K application	Pre-K enrollment	Kindergarten enrollment	Other preschool	Volunteer home visitor	Referral to specialty services	Other	Conclude services

Group Attendance Form

Group No.: _____   Teacher: _____   Location/Phone: _____   Begin date: _____

(P=Present, A= Absent, L=Late, 1/2= Present for only 1/2 of session)

Names (1) Child (2) Adult																							
1																							
2																							
1																							
2																							
1																							
2																							
1																							
2																							
1																							
2																							
1																							
2																							
1																							
2																							
1																							
2																							

Medical Connectedness Rating Scale
Refugee Families Program–Travelers & Immigrants Aid/Erikson Institute

Relevant Parent(s): _____

Family ID No.: _____

Date of Ratings: _____

Objective: Parents will demonstrate increased connectedness to medical and other family support services

	Scale		
Objective	1. Low Level of Development	3. Partially Developed	5. High Level of Development
a. Awareness of medical needs with motive to act	1. Often ignores serious medical needs. Puts no priority on action	3. Unevenly aware of medical needs or only aware of some family member	5. Highly sensitive to medical needs of all family members
b. Understands and accepts Western medicine	1. Almost no understanding or acceptance of Western medical standards and procedures	3. Partial understanding and acceptance of Western medical standards and procedures	5. High level of understanding and acceptance of Western medical standards and procedures
c. Willingness to engage adequate medical resources	1. No clear willingness	3. Sometimes has motive, sometimes does not	5. Very strong motive to engage adequate medical resources
d. Knowledge of and connection with general medical resources	1. Has no knowledge or connection	3. Partial knowledge or connection	5. Has knowledge and connection with a general medical facility
e. Autonomy. Dependency on project for getting medical assistance	1. Low level of autonomy. Does not satisfy a–d	3. Partial autonomy	5. Fully autonomous. Does not need project assistance

D Program Evaluation and Evaluation Instruments

This appendix addresses the impact of the Refugee Families Program (RFP) on children and parents.

The analysis is divided into three areas of evaluation:

I. Impact of the program on the young children enrolled in the child-parent classes.

II. The subsequent public school achievement of children who had been enrolled in the child-parent classes.

III. The impact of the program on parents involved in the child-parent classes.

I. Impact of the program on the young children enrolled in the child-parent classes

In what ways and to what degrees did the children in the child-parent classes improve during the course of the experience in the classes?

Method of Measurement

The instrument used to record changes in the young children who attended the child-parent classes is called the Child Checklist (see example at end of this Appendix). The checklist was developed collaboratively by Erikson staff (Scheinfeld, Wallach, Soroker, and Allen) and the director and teachers of the Refugee Families Program. It is a 73-item instrument, covering 15 areas of the children's growth and development:

1. Social uses of English language (nine items)
2. Early literacy (eight items)
3. Numbers (five items)

4. Letters (two items)
5. Shapes and puzzles (three items)
6. Colors (four items)
7. Animals and human body (four items)
8. Classification, opposites, sequence, and size relation (six items)
9. Rudimentary school disciplines (eight items)
10. Discipline and order (four items)
11. Task orientation (three items)
12. Use of tools and materials (five items)
13. Expressing meaning and pleasure in school learning (five items)
14. Initiative/self-expression (five items)
15. Self-management and hygiene (two items)

The items were identified by the RFP teachers and director as objectives for the child-parent classes. A number of sources inspired the items for the checklist: The Child Assessment Profile of the Chicago Public Schools Early Childhood Programs (1989), CedsitII, a math assessment profile developed by the Erikson Institute Math Project, and the teachers' own list of objectives.

Each item was rated on a four-point scale:

1. Not yet developing, no sign of it.
2. Beginning to be developed, initial signs.
3. Partially developed but fluctuates.
4. Well developed and very strong and consistent aspect of the child's actions/capacities.

For many of the items, the precise meanings of points on the scale are further specified on the instrument.

Entry ratings were made by the teacher of the child-parent class at the end of the child's first month of participation in the class. If at that time, the teacher had not yet been able to observe a particular behavior, the teacher placed a temporary zero (for no chance to observe) and later entered a rating (along with a date of observation) when an opportunity to observe the behavior occurred. A second set of ratings, exit ratings, were made shortly after the child completed his or her class cycle.

In most cases, teachers used separate rating forms for entry and exit ratings. Therefore, when making the exit ratings, they were not looking at the ratings that they had made on the entry checklist.

Table 1
Ratings for Cycles 2–7
(March 1991–July 1995)

Cycle	(No. of Months)	Number of Cases
2	(5.5)	14
3	(5.5)	20
4	(5.5)	10
5	(5.5)	12
6	(9.5)	19
7	(9.5)	18
Total		93

Note that cycles 6–7 are longer than cycles 2–5. The reasons for this change are discussed in chapters 3 and 12.

In the first part of the project's history (cycles 2–5) children often were enrolled in a second cycle of classes when teachers concluded that the child needed further help prior to entering kindergarten. In such cases, only the checklist data for the child's first cycle are included in this analysis. In other words, we have avoided double-counting of children who repeated the classes.

The Child Checklist data analysis reported below was processed in the following way:

First step: The items within each of the sections of the checklist (e.g., Social Uses of English, Literacy, Colors, etc.) were subjected to a principal component analysis to confirm that they were statistically interrelated. Items that did not form a factor with the other items in the group were taken out of that group and placed with items in another section of the interview that more closely corresponded to the item's meaning. For example, item 310, "Writes numbers on own initiative or from verbal directive," was not related to the other items in the numbers section. It was statistically related to the items in the Initiative/Self-expression section, however, and also logically fit into that category.

Second step: The ratings for the items within each section of the interview were averaged. Thus, for example, the entry scores, the exit scores, and the gains (from entry to exit) on the ten items within the "Social Uses of English" section are analyzed as one figure. In the averaging process allowance is made for the variations in the number of subjects reported from one item to another. Thus, for example, because subjects were dropped who had an entry rating of four on any particular variable, the number of subjects reported for one variable may well be different from the number of subjects reported for next variable.

The decision to average the item scores within the sections of the checklist was made for two reasons: First, the averaging of items within each section reduces the likelihood of chance findings that can occur when each item is treated separately. Second, the averaging procedure avoids the problem of overwhelming the reader with separate data on 73 variables.

Table 2 shows the mean gains on the child Checklist across cycles 2–7 of the program for 91 children. Column (2), mean entry rating for the items in this section of the checklist; column (3), mean exit ratings for the items in this section of the checklist; column (4), mean gain from entry ratings to exit ratings; and column (5) indicates whether the difference between the entry and exit scores are statistically significant. In order to arrive at a significance figure, the scale ratings were subject to the Rasch procedure (Linacre and Wright, 1993). The Rasch procedure is designed to deal with the fact that the scales from one item to another are different from each other in two ways: (1) Item scales differ in the difficulty of moving one point on a scale. For example, it is easier to move several points on item 101 (Tells first name) than it is on item 121 (Repeats English words when prompted). It is more difficult to make major gains on the latter than it is on the former. (2) Since the four-point scales represent qualitative ratings we cannot be sure that the intervals between the points on the scale are quantitatively equal. Hence, it is necessary to use a procedure to create a scale that embraces all the items within a category and creates an equal mathematical distance between the points on the scale. The Rasch analysis, which compensates for these two deficits, was used prior to calculating the significance figures.

Column (6) of Table 2 reports how much of the potential gain on the checklist was actually achieved. For example, children who have an entry rating of 1 have the possibility of gaining three points on the four-point scale. By contrast, children who have an entry rating of 3 have the possibility of gaining only 1 point on the scale. The analysis is reported in terms of percentages. For example, a child who starts with a rating of 1 on the four-point scale and exits with a rating of 2 has achieved 33 percent of his or her potential gain. A child who enters with a 3 and ends up with a 4 has achieved 100 percent of the potential gain.

Finally, column (7) of Table 2 answers the question, How do we determine that the reported improvement might not have occurred simply as a function of maturation? This type of question is normally approached through the use of an external control group of children who do not receive the learning opportunity. Since an external control was not feasible in this program (for reasons discussed in the conclusion of this appendix) we have utilized what is, in effect, an *internal* control group. In effect, we are comparing the exit score of a child of a particular age (for example, 48 months) with the entry score of a child who entered the program at the same age (i.e., 48 months). If the first child's exit score significantly exceeds the second child's entry score, then we can assume that the gains shown on the checklist cannot be due simply to maturation.

The analysis was achieved in three steps. In the first step, we used a linear regression analysis in which the dependent variable was the combined entry score for a section of the checklist (e.g., Social Uses of English) as processed through the Rasch analysis. The independent variable is the age of each child at the time the entry ratings were made.

In the second step, we used the result of the first step (Beta coefficient) to predict the exit score of each child based on the child's age at the time of exiting the program. In the third step, we statistically ask whether the children's exit scores significantly exceeds the predicted exit scores. If the significance figure in column (7) is .05 or less (for example, .02) then we can conclude that the mean gain reported in column (4) cannot be explained simply by maturation.

The results given in Table 2 show statistically significant gains in 14 of the 15 areas of learning and development (cols. [4] and [5]). The area that does not show a statistically significant gain (although it shows a gain in the raw scores) is Self-management and Hygiene. It is made up of two items; ''Takes care of personal belongings" and "Is physically clean when comes to group (body, clothing)." The lack of statistically significant gain is probably due to the fact that the average *entry* score on "Physically clean when comes to group" was 3.69 (out of a possible 4), leaving little room for significant gain.

Column (6) shows that the percentage of potential gains achieved in the 15 checklist areas ranges from 45 to 77 percent. Column (7) shows that none of the gains reported in column (5) could be explained as due to the effects of maturation alone.

Table 3 compares the gains in cycles 2–5 (5.5 months each) with the gains in cycles 6–7 (9.5 months each). All but areas 13 (Expressing meaning and pleasure in school learning) and 15 (Self-management and hygiene) show significant increments of gain accompanying the longer (9.5 month) cycles.

Table 4 provides a look at gains in the Child Checklist data from a global perspective that is different from the analysis reported in Tables 2 and 3. Table 4 asks the question: On what percentage of the 73 items did the average child gain one or more points?

Table 4 shows that the average child had the possibility of improving one or more points on an average of 57 items (this is less than 73 items because on each item a percentage of children had entry scores of 4, the top of the scale, that precluded further gains).

The average child actually improved one or more points on 41 items. In other words, the average child improved one or more points on 72 percent of the items on which it was possible to improve.

II. Subsequent public school achievement of children who had been enrolled in the child-parent classes

Teacher Interview Procedures

Methods of Measurement: In 1994 and 1995 the public school teachers of 36 children (18 pre-K or kindergarten and 18 in first or second grade) who had previously participated in RFP child-parent classes were interviewed with the use of *two instruments*: The Follow-Up Checklist and the School Performance Sorting Task. The teachers were distributed across four public elementary schools serving these refugee populations.

Table 2
Mean Gains in Fifteen Areas of the Child Checklist, Cycles 2–7

Area (1)	Mean Entry Score (2)	Mean Exit Score (3)	Mean Gain (4)	Significance of Difference between Entry and Exit* (5)	Percent Made of Potential Gain (6)	Chance of Maturation Explanation* (7)
1. Social uses of English	2.15	3.30	1.15	.000	65	.000
2. Early literacy	1.93	3.06	1.13	.000	59	.000
3. Numbers	2.04	3.24	1.20	.000	65	.000
4. Letters	1.86	2.81	.96	.000	51	.000
5. Shapes and puzzles	2.01	3.26	1.25	.000	66	.000
6. Colors	2.01	3.45	1.44	.000	77	.000
7. Animals and human body	1.88	3.10	1.22	.000	60	.000
8. Classification, opposites, sequence, and size relation	2.00	3.05	1.05	.000	57	.000
9. Rudimentary school disciplines	2.62	3.45	.83	.000	63	.000
10. Discipline and order	2.52	3.40	.88	.000	63	.000
11. Task orientation	2.35	3.13	.78	.000	49	.000
12. Use of tools and materials	2.42	3.14	.72	.000	48	.000
13. Expressing meaning and pleasure in school learning	2.62	3.56	.93	.000	71	.000
14. Initiative/Self-expression	2.05	2.91	.86	.000	47	.000
15. Self-management and hygiene	2.56	3.20	.64	.220	45	.000

Note: N = 91 (cases with entry ratings of 4 for a particular item were dropped from the analysis for that item).
*The figure .000 signifies a very high level of significance, which means that there is .000 possibility that the gain could have happened by chance (col. [5]) or by maturation (col. [7]). On the other hand, the significance figure of .22 in col. (5) signifies a high probability that the reported gain occurred by chance.

Table 3
Comparison of Gains Made during 5.5 Month Cycles (2–5)
with Gains Made during 9.5 Month Cycles (6–7)

Area (1)	Gain in 5.5 Month Cycles ($N = 56$) (2)	Gain in 9.5 Month Cycles ($N = 37$) (3)	Difference between Gains in 5.5 Month Cycles and 9.5 Month Cycles (4)	Significance* (5)
1. Social uses of English	1.05	1.28	.23	.02
2. Early literacy	.99	1.33	.34	.00
3. Numbers	1.03	1.43	.40	.00
4. Letters	.82	1.08	.26	.00
5. Shapes and puzzles	1.07	1.52	.45	.01
6. Colors	1.28	1.65	.37	.01
7. Animals and human body	.96	1.59	.63	.00
8. Classification, opposites, sequence, and size relation	.91	1.27	.36	.01
9. Rudimentary school disciplines	.76	.94	.18	.05
10. Discipline and order	.85	.93	.08	.01
11. Task orientation	.68	.93	.25	.04
12. Use of tools and materials	.53	1.01	.48	.00
13. Expressing meaning and pleasure in school learning	.91	.96	.05	.18
14. Initiative/Self-expression	.75	1.02	.27	.00
15. Self-management and hygiene	.53	.83	.31	.21

*All but items 13 and 15 show a high level of significance for the differences reported between the gains made in the 5.5 month cycles and the 9.5 month cycles.

Table 4
Percentage of Items on Which the Average
Child Improved One or More Points

Average number of items on which the average child *could* improve one or more points: 57
Number of items on which the average child *actually* improved one or more points: 41
Percentage of potential improvement realized in actual improvement: 72% (41/57)

Follow-Up Checklist: The purpose of the Follow-Up Check-list is to construct a profile of how an RFP graduate is per-forming in public school based on his or her public school teacher's rating of the child on a wide range of school relevant dimensions. The instrument has 71 items on the pre-K/kinder-garten form and 70 items on the first/second grade form. The first/second grade form drops items that are suited mainly to pre-K/kindergarten children and adds items that cover performance in language arts and math. A four-point scale is used in the Follow-Up Checklist: (1) not yet developed, no sign of it; (2) beginning to be developed, initial signs of it now; (3) moderately developed; and (4) well-developed, very strong, and consistent aspect of child's actions and capacities.

The instrument section at the end of this appendix lists the items covered in the two forms of the Follow-Up Checklist. The complete instruments could not be included because of space limitations. Copies of the Follow-Up Checklist are avail-able from the authors upon request (Daniel Scheinfeld, Erikson Institute, 420 North Wabash, Chicago, IL 60611).

School Performance Sorting Task: The teacher was presented with a pack of 4" × 6" printed cards containing a card for each child in her classroom. The cards were filled out by the interviewer, using the class roster, at the beginning of the interview. For each of the 14 dimensions of school performance listed on the cards, the teacher was asked to sort the children of the class into three piles (below average in the class, average in the class, and above average in the class). Fourteen separate sorts were involved in this procedure:

- English language use
- Conceptual development (pre-K/kindergarten only)

- Social-emotional development
- School behavior
- Discipline and order
- Task orientation
- Fine motor skills
- Motivation
- Gross motor skills (pre-K/kindergarten only)
- Self-management
- Hygiene
- Dress
- Attendance
- Parent involvement
- Language arts (first and second grades only)
- Math (first and second grades only)

After a sort, each child's card was marked by the interviewer with the number of the pile into which it had been sorted by the teacher: below average, 1; average, 2; and above average, 3.

Table 5 gives the results of this teacher sorting process for 18 pre-K and kindergarten children who are RFP graduates and compares their rankings to their classmates. Column (2) lists the mean ranking score of the eighteen RFP graduates on fourteen areas of school performance. Column (3) gives the mean ranking score of the classmates of the RFP graduates. Column (4) provides the difference between columns (2) and (3).

Table 5 shows that the RFP graduates had appreciably higher average ranking on social-emotional development, school behavior, discipline/order, fine motor skills, and attendance. They had an appreciably lower score in dress.

Table 6 provides us with some additional information regarding the meaning of the figures in Table 5. Column (2) lists the ranking scores yielded by the School Performance Sorting Tasks for the 18 RFP graduates. These are the same figures that are found in column (2) of Table 5. They refer to the average ranking of the 18 RFP graduates on the teacher sorting tasks (1, below average; 2, average; and 3, above average). Column (3) shows the averaged scores from the Follow-Up Checklist data that related to the same fourteen areas of school performance as those covered by sort task. Thus, for example, in column (2), the 18 RFP graduates had an average ranking in their class of 1.83 out of a possible 3, on English

Table 5
Comparison of Prekindergarten and Kindergarten Teacher Rankings of RFP Graduates with Teacher Rankings of Classmates on School Performance Sorting Task

Area (1)	Mean Teacher Rankings of RFP Graduates* (N = 18) (2)	Mean Teacher Rankings of Classmates of RFP Graduates* (N=205) (3)	Difference between RFP Graduates and Their Classmates (4)
1. English language	1.83	1.92	−.09
2. Conceptual development	2.11	1.97	.14
3. Social-emotional development	2.61	2.14	.47
4. School behavior	2.61	2.18	.43
5. Discipline/order	2.61	2.16	.45
6. Task orientation	2.22	2.08	.14
7. Fine motor skills	2.39	2.12	.27
8. Motivation	2.17	2.10	.07
9. Gross motor skills	2.56	2.44	.12
10. Self-management	2.00	2.12	.12
11. Hygiene	2.22	2.38	−.16
12. Dress	2.11	2.40	−.29
13. Attendance	3.00	2.44	.56
14. Parent involvement	2.11	2.00	.11

*Figures based on teacher ranking of each child in the class as 1, below average in the class; 2, average in the class; or 3, above average in the class.

language. On the Follow-Up Checklist there are three items relating to the English language dimension:

- 100: Understands simple directives and requests in English
- 101: Language ability in English compared to American born children his/her age
- 102: Attitude toward learning new words in English

Each of these three items was rated by the teacher on a 4-point scale on the Follow-Up Checklist. The average rating for the eighteen RFP graduates on a scale which averages these three scales is 3.17 out of a possible 4.00.

On the discipline/order dimension, the 18 RFP graduates had an average ranking (col. [2]) of 2.61 in the teacher sort. On the Follow-Up Checklist, there are three items corresponding to this dimension:

- 501: Comfortably follows classroom rules, routines, and structure of the day
- 502: Responds to teacher requests and directions
- 503: Accepts teacher limitations on an activity without withdrawing or acting out

The RFP graduates' average ratings on these three dimensions on the Follow-Up Checklist was 3.38 (out of a possible 4).

If we average the column (3) Follow-Up Checklist scores for dimensions 1–13 (not including parent involvement) we get an average score of 3.49 out of a possible 4.00 as an indicator of the 18 RFP graduates' school adaptation. This figure speaks well for their pre-K/kindergarten performance.

Tables 7 and 8 provide data on another 18 RFP graduates. These children were in *first and second grade* at the time that the School Performance Sorting Task and the Follow-Up Checklist were administered to their public school teachers. Table 7 and 8 are constructed in the same manner as Tables 5 and 6, e.g., see the above discussion preceding Table 6 in order to understand the construction of Table 8. The difference is that these are RFP graduates who have been in public school somewhat longer than the preschoolers and kindergartners reported in Tables 5 and 6. Table 7 suggests that these 18 RFP graduates, rated by their first- and second-grade public teachers, have *appreciably* higher ranking than their public school classmates on school behavior, discipline/order, task orientation, motivation, and attendance. They are *somewhat* higher than their public school classmates on social-emotional development, fine motor skills, self-management, hygiene, and parent involvement. They are roughly equal with their public school classmates in English language, language arts, and math.

In Table 8, if we average the Follow-Up Checklist scores in column (3) (leaving off parent involvement) we see an average score of 3.44 out of a possible 4.00 as an indicator of the school adaptation of these first- and second-grade RFP graduates. As

Table 6
Public School Follow-Up Checklist Ratings
Corresponding to Prekindergarten and Kindergarten
Teachers' Rankings of RFP Graduates on School
Performance Sorting Task (N=18)

Area (1)	Mean Teacher Rankings of RFP Graduates* (2)	Mean Teacher Ratings on Corresponding Groups of Items in Follow-Up Checklist** (3)
1. English language	1.83	3.17 (out of 4)
2. Conceptual development	2.11	3.10
3. Emotional development	2.61	3.27
4. School behavior	2.61	2.43
5. Discipline/order	2.61	3.38
6. Task orientation	2.22	3.22
7. Fine motor skills	2.39	3.57
8. Motivation	2.17	3.17
9. Gross motor skills	2.56	3.89
10. Self-management	2.00	3.93
11. Hygiene	2.22	3.76
12. Dress	2.11	3.50
13. Attendance	3.00	4.00
14. Parent involvement	2.11	3.67

*Figures based on teacher ranking of each child in the class as 1, below average in the class; 2, average in the class; or 3, above average in the class.
**Figures based on four-point scale.

with the younger RFP graduates, the figure speaks well for their school adaptation.

III. Impact of the program on parents involved in the child-parent classes

In what ways and to what degrees did the parents in the child-parent classes improve during the course of the experience in the classes? Further, how much of the potential gain on the parent checklists was actually achieved?

Method of Measurement: The instrument used to record changes in the parents who attended the child-parent classes is called The Parent-Child Checklist (see example at end of

Table 7
Comparison of First and Second Grade Teacher Rankings of RFP Graduates with Teacher Rankings of Classmates on School Performance Sorting Task

Area (1)	Mean Teacher Rankings of RFP Graduates* (N=18) (2)	Mean Teacher Rankings of Classmates of RFP Graduates* (N=122) (3)	Difference between RFP Graduates and Their Classmates (4)
1. English language	1.89	1.81	.08
2. Social-emotional development	2.17	1.87	.30
3. School behavior	2.44	1.92	.52
4. Discipline/order	2.44	1.93	.51
5. Task orientation	2.39	1.85	.54
6. Fine motor skills	2.33	2.02	.31
7. Motivation	2.39	1.91	.48
8. Self-management	2.22	1.90	.32
9. Hygiene	2.39	2.14	.25
10. Dress	2.56	2.21	.35
11. Attendance	2.83	2.35	.48
12. Parent involvement	2.22	2.00	.22
13. Language arts	1.94	1.97	.03
14. Math	2.22	2.12	.10

*Figures based on teacher ranking of each child in the class as 1, below average in the class; 2, average in the class; or 3, above average in the class.

this Appendix). The checklist is similar in structure to the Child-Child Checklist and also was developed collaboratively by Erikson staff and the staff of the Refugee Families Program. It is a 33-item instrument, covering eight areas of the parents' growth and development as observed by the teachers: (1) parent availability to child; (2) parent participation in child's learning activities; (3) parent giving child space to do and learn things on his or her own; (4) parent positive reinforcement of child's learning; (5) parent in relation to child's play; (6) parent role in child's disruptive behavior; (7) parent as learner; and

Table 8
Public School Follow-Up Checklist Ratings
Corresponding to First and Second Grade Teachers'
Rankings of RFP Graduates on School Performance
Sorting Task (N=18)

Area (1)	Mean Teacher Rankings of RFP Graduates (2)	Mean Teacher Ratings on Corresponding Groups of Items in Follow-Up Checklist (3)
1. English language	1.89	3.61
2. Social-emotional development	2.17	3.30
3. School behavior	2.44	3.69
4. Discipline/order	2.44	3.57
5. Task orientation	2.39	3.26
6. Fine motor skills	2.33	3.86
7. Motivation	2.39	3.39
8. Self-management	2.22	3.39
9. Hygiene	2.39	3.67
10. Dress	2.56	3.61
11. Attendance	2.83	4.00
12. Parent involvement	2.22	3.46
13. Language arts	1.94	2.31
14. Math	2.22	3.00

Note: See discussion preceding Table 6 for an explanation of cols. (2) and (3).

(8) parent's cooperation with the class process. In addition, a ninth area on the checklist covered child's behavioral indicators of parent-child relationship. This category includes two items: child stays on task in caregiver's absence, and child and caregiver capable of working in collaboration.

The format for the 33 items is a four-point scale:

1. Not present at all in the parent's actions
2. Slight signs of this
3. Fairly strong signs of this, but fluctuates
4. Very strong and consistent signs of this in parent's actions

Entry ratings were made by the teacher of each class at the end of the parent's first month of participation in the classes. Exit ratings were made shortly after the end of the cycle.

As with the Child Checklist, teachers normally used a separate rating form for entry and exit ratings. Therefore, when making the exit ratings they were not looking at the ratings that they had made on the entry checklist.

The analysis of the Parent-Child Checklist data was conducted in the same manner as that reported for Child Checklist data reported in Table 2 above. In arriving at calculations of significance, the Rasch procedure was used to create a scale that combines all the items within a category (e.g., within the category of parent availability to the child) and creates equal mathematical distance between the points on the scale.

Table 9 provides data on the amount of gain made by 71 parents as rated by the teachers on the Parent-Child Checklist. The analysis groups the 33 items of the instrument into nine categories, following the categories set down in the instrument itself (see below). Note that the average entry ratings for parents show figures that are somewhere between a rating of 2 ("slight signs of this") and a rating of 3 ("fairly strong signs of this but fluctuates"). On virtually all of the dimensions the average parent ratings moved into the level of showing "fairly strong signs." All but two of the gains figures are statistically significant.

The question posed by Table 10 is: Did the parents make greater improvements in the 9.5 month cycles than in the 5.5 month cycles? In six of the nine areas of parent development we see a statistically significant increment in the average parent gains reported for the longer, 9.5 month cycles. This accompanies the similar gain increments made by their children during the longer cycles. While the increments are modest, they support the staff's decision to lengthen the periods of class exposure.

Summary of the Findings

Child Checklists (Tables 2–4)

The data as a whole show that the 91 children involved in the Child Checklist analysis for cycles 2–7 made statistically significant gains in fourteen of the fifteen areas of learning

Table 9
Mean Gains of Parents in the Nine Areas of the Parent Checklist, Cycles 2–7. N = 68 (Cases with entry of 4 on any particular item were dropped from the analysis for that particular item)

Area (1)	Mean Entry Score* (2)	Mean Exit Score* (3)	Mean Gain (4)	Significance of Difference between Entry and Exit** (5)	Percent Made of Potential Gain (6)
1. Parent availability to child	2.56	3.11	.55	***	
2. Parent participation in child's learning activities	2.35	2.96	.61	.00	39%
3. Parent giving child space to do and learn things on his/her own	2.57	3.15	.59	.00	42%
4. Parent positive reinforcement of child's learning	2.41	2.98	.57	.00	36%
5. Parent in relation to child's play	2.43	3.07	.64	.00	44%
6. Parent role in child's social development	2.52	31.4	.62	.36	45%
7. Parent as learner	2.39	3.08	.70	.20	42%
8. Parent cooperation with the class process	2.63	3.22	.59	.00	45%
9. Child's behavioral indicators of parent-child relationship (child stays on task in parent's absence and child and parent capable of working in collaboration)	2.54	3.35	.81	.01	56%

*Figures based on four-point scale.
**.000 means that there is .000 possibility that the gain could have happened by chance.
***The Rasch analysis, which restructures the scales as discussed above, shows that in its terms there was a slight decline in the score for the Parent Availability category, even though the raw scores reflect a slight increase.

Table 10
Comparison of Gains on the Parent-Child Checklist Made during the 5.5 Month Cycles (2–5) with Gains Made during the 9.5 Month Cycles (6–7)

Area (1)	Gain in 5.5 Month Cycles ($N = 43$) (2)	Gain in 9.5 Month Cycles ($N = 25$) (3)	Difference between Gains in 5.5 Month Cycles and 9.5 Month Cycles (4)	Significance* (5)
1. Parent availability to child	.41	.70	.29	.00
2. Parent participation in child's learning activities	.49	.78	.30	.00
3. Parent giving child space to do and learn things on his/her own	.47	.75	.28	.00
4. Parent positive reinforcement of child's learning	.42	.78	.36	.02
5. Parent in relation to child's play	.45	.87	.41	.00
6. Parent role in child's social development	.52	.73	.21	.10
7. Parent as learner	.59	.83	.24	.02
8. Parent cooperation with the class process	.55	.65	.10	.11
9. Child's behavioral indicators of parent-child relationship (child stays on task in parent's absence and child and parent capable of working in collaboration)	.80	.85	.05	.09

*All but items 6, 8, and 9 show a high level of significance for the difference reported between gains made in the 5.5 month cycles and the 9.5 month cycles.

and development (Table 2). There is an average gain of more than one scale point for seven of those fourteen areas. The gains in the other seven areas range from .72 to .96 scale points. It is important to note that in all but two of the fifteen areas the average exit scores were greater than 3.0 (out of a possible 4.0). Further, the gains reported in Table 2 cannot be explained simply as a function of maturation (col. [7]). The advantages resulting from lengthening the cycles from 5.5 months to 9.5 months (Table 3) are modest but significant.

In the global analysis (Table 4) the average child moved one point or more on 72 percent of items on which it was possible to move.

Public School Follow-Up Study (Tables 5–8)

The public school teacher-sort data on the 18 RFP graduates who were at the pre-K and kindergarten level at the time of the survey show that the RFP graduates were appreciably higher than their public school classmates in four areas: social-emotional development, school behavior, discipline/order, and attendance. (Table 5) It is interesting to note that these four areas all cover personal behavior patterns and dispositions that support school achievement rather than concept and skill development. We see the same pattern in Table 7, relating to the 18 RFP graduates who were at the first- and second-grade level at the time of the survey. In the areas that involve language and conceptual development, on the other hand, the RFP graduates of both samples are only at par or slightly higher than their classmates. These areas include English language and conceptual development for pre-K/kindergarten grades and English language, language arts, and math for first- and second-graders (Tables 5 and 7).

Parent-Child Checklist (Tables 9 and 10)

The average *entry* ratings on the nine areas of the Parent-Child Checklist (cycles 2–7) show figures that are somewhere between 2 ("slight signs of this") and 3 ("fairly strong signs of this, but fluctuates"). The entry average across these nine areas is 2.49 (Table 9). The average *exit* rating across the nine areas is 3.12 (slightly above the 3.0 level of "fairly strong signs of this, but fluctuates"). These findings suggest substantial gains but also significant room for improvement. The percentage of potential gain made for the nine areas averaged together is 39 percent.

The increments of progress on the Parent-Child Checklist between the longer cycles (9.5 months) and the shorter cycles (5.5 months) are statistically significant on six of the nine dimensions (parent availability to child, parent's participation in child's learning activities, parent giving child space to work on his or her own, parent's positive reinforcement of child's learning, parent's relation to child's play, and parent as learner (Table 10). The average advantage of the 9.5 cycles over the 5.5 cycles for these six areas is .31 of a scale point. This difference is modest but supports the RFP staff's overall observation that the lengthening of the cycles was well conceived.

Methodological Notes

This addendum provides a set of reflections on the overall design of the evaluation. In many respects it is similar to Chapter 12, in which we addressed issues in the design of the Refugee Family Program as a whole. Our intent in this discussion is to explore aspects of the evaluation design that are of concern to us and may interest the reader.

In the best of all possible worlds, our approach to measuring the impact of the child-parent classes on children's learning and development would have involved multiple measures of the children's progress. A basic methodological principle of evaluation design is that the use of multiple measures, ideally rendered by multiple investigators, significantly contributes to the overall strength of the findings. Why then did we rely solely on a teacher checklist that, in addition to being a single measure, raises questions concerning the "objectivity" of the ratings since teachers ostensibly have an investment in seeing the progress of their pupils? For example, the strength of the evaluation clearly would have been greater if our approach had included measurements rendered by outside observers or testers. This issue was with us from the earliest phase of the evaluation design. For a number of reasons, the circumstances involved in this program mitigated against the use of outside data testers or observers. First, it is widely perceived that testing is usually not an appropriate measurement procedure for children of preschool age. In our estimation and that of the RFP staff, a testing regimen, rendered by outside evaluators, would have been particularly inappropriate for refugee children, most of whom spoke virtually no English at the point of entry and many of whom were shy of strangers. Second, the introduction of a formal testing regimen would also have been highly disruptive to the delicate process involved in teachers bridging cultural, social, and linguistic barriers to form relationships with the children and parents in the classes. An alternative strategy might have been the use of outside observers to record children's behavior. Our explorations into this possibility convinced us that a reliable set of findings would have required very frequent participation by observers in the classes in order to cover a significant set of variables in a reliable fashion. This also would have been highly intrusive.

In retrospect, while appreciating that our choice was largely dictated by the circumstances described above, we are still keenly aware of the limitations of a single measure confined to teacher ratings. In our view, the use of teacher ratings is a strong form of measurement even given the acknowledge limitations. No one has the possibility of the multiple observations and consequent knowledge of a child that is available to a teacher. On the other hand, it would have been clearly desirable to have had a second set of measures.

A further question concerns our decision to develop our own checklist. Given that we decided to limit ourselves to teacher-rendered measures, why did we not use a standardized child checklist that would have allowed us to compare the RFP children to other populations of children? Our decision to create the Child Checklist was governed significantly by the ideals of collaboration that underpinned our relationship with the RFP staff. The items used on the Child Checklist reflect the particular objectives of the program staff, articulated during the formative stage of the program. No instrument of which we were aware provided that kind of one-to-one coverage. In retrospect, a thorough consideration of the advantages of utilizing a standardized instrument checklist might have altered our decision, depending upon the availability of a suitable instrument.

Finally, it is evident that the evaluation design would have been stronger with the inclusion of an external control group;

i.e., measures taken on a group of children who were not served by the program, but who reflected the same cultural and SES backgrounds as the children served in the program. Given the nature of the program and its relationship with the client population, we concluded, albeit regretfully, that the possibility of constructing and measuring a control group in a valid and reliable manner was not a practical option. First, for moral, spiritual, and professional reasons, the staff of the Refugee Families Program was strongly opposed to excluding families from child-parent classes for purposes of constructing a control group. Furthermore, the prospect of identifying and gaining access to 20–25 Cambodian families and another 15 Vietnamese families with young children who were not participating in the program but who shared the attributes of the families in the program was highly unlikely. The main areas of refugee settlement in Chicago were the neighborhoods being served by the RFP. Further, the use of a control group no doubt would have required some kind of testing procedure, which we have ruled out in the above discussion. As an alternative to utilizing an external control group, we have constructed an *internal* control group as described in the above discussion regarding column (7) of Table 2. The internal control is, in our estimation, a useful innovation that has served us well.

Evaluation Instruments

Child Checklist*
Refugee Families Program
TIA/Erikson Institute

1. Family I.D. number: __ __ __/__ __
                              Family Number Culture Group

   Culture Group Key: 01=Cambodian, 02=Laotian, 03=
   Vietnamese, 04=Ethiopian (Amharic), 05=Somali, 06=
   Eritrean, 07=Afghan, 08=Chinese-Vietnamese

2. Child's program I.D. number: __ __/__ __/__ __ __/__
                                  Cycle   Group Family No. Child

- -

(TIA staff please fill out below. Erikson fills out 1 and 2
above.)

Basic Data on Child:

3. Child's name: _____

   13. Rater for column A: _____.
   (1=Lisa Rademacher, 2=Lisa Bangs, 3=Trudi)
   14. Date of ratings for column A: __/__/__.
   15. Rater for column B: _____
   16. Date of ratings for column B: __/__/__.
   17. Rater for column C: _____
   18. Date of ratings for column C: __/__/__.
   19. Rater for column D: _____
   20. Date of ratings for column D: __/__/__.

Key to ratings on checklist:
   0 = No chance to observe this (if circumstances are
   exceptional around this 0, please write some explanation in the margin).

*Derived from the Chicago Public Schools (cps) Child Assessment Profile for Early
Childhood Programs: cps3 denotes an item for three-year-olds; cps4, an item for
four-year-olds (Board of Education of the City of Chicago, 1989).

1 = Not yet developing, no sign of it
2 = Beginning to be developed, initial signs
3 = Partially developed but fluctuates
4 = Well developed and very strong and consistent aspect of child's actions/capacities

Key to the four rating columns (A–D) and data on entry dates:
A = *Early in cycle* (third or fourth week).
B = *Observed later in cycle, first chance at accurate reading* (i.e., column A rating not possible). Mark exact week in parentheses next to rating; e.g., "2 (12)" = Data available in twelfth week and child got a rating of 2.
C = *End of nine-month class cycle.* Exact time in weeks: _____.
D = *End of continuation or reconstituted class.* Exact time in weeks from beginning of program involvement: _____.

A. English in Social Interaction

1. English Language/Social Uses

	A	B	C	D	
101.	___	___	___	___	Tells first name (cps3).
104a.	___	___	___	___	Calls teacher by appropriate name (e.g., "teacher," first name, etc.; adap. of cps4). 1= calls teacher nothing, 2=calls teacher something, 3=calls teacher "teacher," 4=calls teacher by proper name.
106.	___	___	___	___	Give greetings and goodbyes.
109.	___	___	___	___	Makes simple requests to teacher.
111.	___	___	___	___	Points to object in picture when named-cps.
113.	___	___	___	___	Names familiar objects (cps3) (refers to English language labeling of objects familiar to child in their own world).

119. ___ ___ ___ ___ Talks with other children in *English* (adap. of cps4) or *Native* language (adap. of cps4).

121a. ___ ___ ___ ___ Repeats English words when prompted.

122. ___ ___ ___ ___ Repeats English words without prompting.

123. ___ ___ ___ ___ Native Language Rating (2 pt. scale): Apparent capacity of child to speak in native language (1 = appears to be subnormal, problematic; 2 = appears to be average or better).

124. ___ ___ ___ ___ English Language Rating compared to American children his/her age. (1 = no apparent capacity in English; 2 = beginning vocabulary with single words; 3 = fairly developed capacity to understand and speak with single words and short phrases; 4 = understands and speaks in whole sentences or understands most conversations with teacher and initiates English conversation.)

- -

B. Conceptual/Language Development

2. Early Literacy

    A   B   C   D

203. ___ ___ ___ ___ Repeats song, rhymes, and fingerplays while being presented in class session (adap. of cps4).

205. ____ ____ ____ ____   Produces recognizable drawing of objects (i.e., some communication of ideas through drawing).

208. ____ ____ ____ ____   Shows that he/she recognizes the existence of letters (e.g., can recognize some letters when they are named or can name some letters).

209. ____ ____ ____ ____   Recognizes first letter of name.

210. ____ ____ ____ ____   Recognizes first name in print.

211. ____ ____ ____ ____   Prints first letter of name.

212. ____ ____ ____ ____   Prints first name.

213. ____ ____ ____ ____   Listens to story (adap. of cps3).

3. Basic Conceptual/Linguistic Development (Using English Language)

Numbers

A   B   C   D

301. ____ ____ ____ ____   Pretend counting—"counts" objects without clear grasp of number meaning, sequence, etc. (1 = no sign; 2 = little bit; 3 = fairly extensive; 4 = not relevant; child can count, goes way beyond this).

302. ____ ____ ____ ____   Gives or takes one to three objects when asked (adap. of cps3).

303. ____ ____ ____ ____   Rote counts (recites number sequence) (1 = not at all; 2 = counts numbers 1 to 3; 3 = 1 to 5; 4 = 1 to 10 or better).

304. ____ ____ ____ ____   One-to-one correspondence: Counts objects accurately when they are previously arranged in a clear sequence. 1 = not at all; 2 = one to three objects

(e.g., three blocks; three pieces of candy); 3 = four to six objects; 4 = seven to ten objects or better.

305. ____ ____ ____ ____ Counts objects accurately when they are all mixed up (not neatly arranged beforehand). 1 = not at all, 2 = two to three objects (e.g., three blocks, three pieces of candy); 3 = one to five; 4 = one to ten.

306a. ____ ____ ____ ____ Recognizes and states written numbers. 1 = not at all; 2 = can identify one to three numbers; 3 = can identify four to six numbers; 4 = can identify seven to ten numbers.

308a. ____ ____ ____ ____ Sight numbers: verbally identifies number of items in a set of objects without explicitly counting (e.g., can verbally identify three dots on a die, five blocks). 1 = not at all; 2 = set of one to three; 3 = set of four to six; 4 = set of seven to ten or better.

310. ____ ____ ____ ____ Writes numbers on own initiative or from verbal directive. 1 = not at all; 2 = one to three numbers; 3 = four to six; 4 = seven to ten.

Letters

311. ____ ____ ____ ____ Recites alphabet song. 1 = not at all; 2 = clusters of three or four letters in correct sequence; 3 = clusters of five to ten in correct sequence; 4 = recites most or all of the alphabet song.

312. ____ ____ ____ ____ Recites alphabet 1 = not at all; 2 = clusters of three or four letters in correct sequence; 3 = clusters of five to ten in correct sequence; 4 = recites most or all of the alphabet in correct sequence.

313a. ____ ____ ____ ____ Writes letters (mid-kindergarten).

314. ____ ____ ____ ____ Creates pretend writing. 1 = not at all; 2 = random scribbles; 3 = scribbles in word clusters; 4 = writes letters.

Shapes

315. ____ ____ ____ ____ Points to four basic shapes when named (circle, square, triangle, rectangle) cps4.

317a. ____ ____ ____ ____ Verbally identifies shapes by self.

319a. ____ ____ ____ ____ Draws shapes (square, rectangle, triangle, circle) cps-4.

Puzzles

321. ____ ____ ____ ____ Part-whole puzzles: 1 = cannot do any part-whole puzzle, no matter how simple; 2 = can do a very simple part-whole puzzle; 3 = can fairly constantly, but not always, put together a middle level part-whole puzzle; 4 = can fairly constantly put together higher level (more complex) part-whole puzzle.

322. ____ ____ ____ ____ Jigsaw puzzle: 1 = cannot do any jigsaw puzzle, no matter how simple; 2 = shows beginnings, perhaps can put two or a few jigsaw pieces together; 3 =

can put together a four to six piece jigsaw puzzle fairly constantly but does get stuck; 4 = can consistently do jigsaw puzzles of six or more pieces.

Colors

327. _____ _____ _____ _____ Matches the three primary colors—red, blue, yellow (i.e., matches two or more objects of each primary color).

328. _____ _____ _____ _____ Points to an object identified by teacher in terms of primary colors.

329. _____ _____ _____ _____ Names objects in terms of the three primary colors—red, blue, yellow (i.e., can look at an object and name its color).

330. _____ _____ _____ _____ Names three or more secondary (other) colors (h/s cps).

Animals (including parts of animal body)

332. _____ _____ _____ _____ Can point to picture of familiar animals (commonly seen in their books, trip to zoo, etc.) when named (CedsitII). 1 = not at all; 2 = one to four animals; 3 = five to ten; 4 = over ten.

333. _____ _____ _____ _____ Names pictures of animals. 1 = not at all; 2 = one to four; 3 = five to ten; 4 = over ten.

Human body

336. _____ _____ _____ _____ Points to human body parts when named (cps3) 1 = not at all; 2 = one to three human body parts; 3 = four to six; 4 = seven or more parts.

337. ____ ____ ____ ____ Names body parts (adap. of cps4) 1 = not at all; 2 = two body parts; 3 = four to five body parts; 4 = six or more body parts.

Classification/sorting

341. ____ ____ ____ ____ Sorts objects by one attribute (e.g., size, color, etc.).

342. ____ ____ ____ ____ Sorts objects by two attributes (e.g., shape and color).

Opposites

344a. ____ ____ ____ ____ Understands opposites such as big/small, hot/cold, dry/wet, short/tall (the understanding is revealed through response to teacher directive or question, in spontaneous statements, or in some other form).

Sequential order

349. ____ ____ ____ ____ Understands concept of first, second, and third.

350. ____ ____ ____ ____ Reproduces a simple two- or three-part pattern as in red-yellow-green bead sequence (Jan Jewett).

Size relation

351. ____ ____ ____ ____ Arranges three objects in sequence of size (cps3).

- -

C. Learning Processes and Disciplines

4. Basic, Rudimentary School Disciplines

     A   B   C   D

401. ____ ____ ____ ____ Sits patiently, watches/waits while being instructed before engaging materials.

402a. ____ ____ ____ ____ Follows simple activity instructions with example. 4 = instructions of 3 or more steps; 3 = instructions of 2 steps; 2 = instructions of 1 step; 1 = not at all.

404. ____ ____ ____ ____ Takes turns with other children *when reminded*.

405. ____ ____ ____ ____ Voluntarily takes turns with other children (i.e., without having to be reminded).

406. ____ ____ ____ ____ Shares materials with other children.

408. ____ ____ ____ ____ Accepts teacher limitations on activity without withdrawing or acting out.

409. ____ ____ ____ ____ Plays/works cooperatively with peers.

412. ____ ____ ____ ____ Helps clean up, replaces materials when end of time period is announced, 1 = not at all, even when reminded; 2 = with further reminding; 3 = sometimes without further reminding, fluctuates; 4 = virtually always without reminding (adap. of cps4).

413. ____ ____ ____ ____ Seeks and uses teacher assistance when needed (adap. of cps3).

505. ____ ____ ____ ____ Respects, takes care of classroom materials (formerly 505).

5. Discipline and Order

      A   B   C   D

502. ____ ____ ____ ____ Responds to teacher requests and directions (implies both understanding and being willing to respond).

503a. ____ ____ ____ ____ Responds to own parent's requests and directions (implies both understanding and being willing to respond).

504. ____ ____ ____ ____ Responds to other parent's requests and directions (implies both understanding and being willing to respond).

506. ____ ____ ____ ____ Respects other children's activities.

508. ____ ____ ____ ____ Plays games that have rules and follows rules (e.g., Bingo, Dominoes, Bluebird) (adap. of cps4).

6. Task Orientation (response to assigned tasks).

      A   B   C   D

601. ____ ____ ____ ____ Works independently on assigned task

602. ____ ____ ____ ____ Concentrates on tasks/not easily distracted

605. ____ ____ ____ ____ Applies effort and quality/integrity to the activities (vs. rushes through, sacrificing quality for speed or completion).

D. Tools, Motor Skills, and Use of Materials

7. Tools, Motor Skills, and Materials of the Classroom

      A   B   C   D

701. ____ ____ ____ ____ Uses pencil, crayons, or marker. 1 = not at all; 2 = by holding and using it with fist; 3 = by crudely holding it with finger and thumb, but not yet very adept; 4 = by holding fairly or very adeptly with finger and thumb—comfortable, natural usage.

704a. ___ ___ ___ ___ Holds scissors and snips with control to cut along wide, straight, and curved lines (cps-4).

705. ___ ___ ___ ___ Uses paste/glue reasonably effectively.

706a. ___ ___ ___ ___ Can use lacing board. 4 = laces in sequence; 3 = laces all over; 2 = laces somewhat; 1 = laces not at all.

712. ___ ___ ___ ___ Strings beads (adap. of cps3 and cps4).

714. ___ ___ ___ ___ Builds complex structures with blocks. 4 = ten or more blocks; 3 = five to ten blocks; 2 = less than five blocks; 1 = not at all.

E. Self as Learner

8. Experiencing Meaning and Pleasure in School and Learning

A   B   C   D

803. ___ ___ ___ ___ Shows interest and enthusiasm in the learning activities.

804. ___ ___ ___ ___ Shows pride in own accomplishments cps3.

805. ___ ___ ___ ___ Feels confident about learning new things.

806. ___ ___ ___ ___ Generally feels comfortable being in the group.

807. ___ ___ ___ ___ Generally enthusiastic about coming to group.

9. Agency/Initiative/Self-expression (child's actual experience of Agency reflected in either assigned tasks or free play)

A   B   C   D

903. ___ ___ ___ ___ Able to make choice (when presented with choice) 1 = not at

all; 2 = on rare occasions; 3 = fairly consistently in some areas (but not all or even most); 4 = consistently across the whole range of classroom choices.

906. ___ ___ ___ ___ Responds well to obstacles (e.g., tries to figure out a way, etc., rather than folding, freezing, angrily rejecting the activity, or leaving the field). 1 = does not respond well at all, folds/withdraws consistently; 2 = on rare occasions will try to figure way out, but usually folds or withdraws; 3 = quite frequently will try to figure a way, but sometimes folds or withdraws; 4 = continually pushes to find ways out of obstacles. Does not fold or withdraw.

909. ___ ___ ___ ___ Initiates activities with other children, engages other children in play (Jan J.).

F. Self-management and Hygiene

10. Self-management
     A   B   C   D

2. ___ ___ ___ ___ Takes care of personal belongings.

11. Hygiene (as reflection of parental care)
     A   B   C   D

1101. ___ ___ ___ ___ Is physically clean when comes to group (body, clothing).

Parent-Child Checklist
Teacher Observation of Parent in Class

1. Family I.D. number: __ __ __/__ __
   Family Number Culture Group

   Culture Group Key: 01=Cambodian, 02=Laotian, 03=
   Vietnamese, 04=Ethiopian (Amharic), 05=Somali, 06=
   Eritrean, 07=Afghan, 08=Chinese-Vietnamese

2. Caregiver I.D. number: __ __/__ __/__ __ __/__
   Cycle Family Culture Relation
   Began No.   to child

- -
(TIA staff please fill out this section.)

3. Caregiver name: _____

4. Caregiver's relation to target child (children) _____

5. Number of children family has in the program: _____

6. Name of child No. 1: _____

7. Name of child No. 2: _____

8. Rater for column A: _____
(1=Lisa Rademacher, 2=Lisa Bangs, 3=Trudi)

9. Date of ratings for column A: __/__/__

10. Rater for column B: _____

11. Date of ratings for column B: __/__/__

12. Rater for column C: _____

13. Date of ratings for column C: __/__/__

14. Rater for column D: _____

15. Date of ratings for column D: __/__/__

Key to Ratings
   0 = No opportunity to observe this.
   1 = Not present at all in parent's actions.
   2 = Slight signs of this. This behavior or capability is
   manifest only from time to time. Caregiver does not display the converse behavior but also does not strongly
   show the positive behavior. Ambivalent.

3 = Fairly strong signs of this, but fluctuates. This behavior or capability is displayed 50–75 percent of the optimum. Parent/child takes advantage of 50–75 percent of all opportunities to display this behavior or capability.

4 = Very strong and consistent signs of this in parent's actions. With only an occasional exception (approximately once every month), this behavior or capability is displayed when the opportunity presents itself. This rating applies when a parent/child has attained close to the best possible, ideal development of this capability or action.

Key to Columns

A = Observed at end of third or fourth week in program.
B = Observed later in cycle (not observable in third or fourth week) (put number of week in which it was observed in parentheses next to rating, e.g., fifth week in cycle = 5).
C = End of nine-month class period.
D = End of nine-month continuation or restructured class.
NA = Assumed behavior not present and question not applicable. For example, in question 601: "Takes responsibility for child's disruptive behavior in class. . . ." If child is never disruptive, caregiver has no opportunity to display this desired behavior and rates NA.

1. Parent Availability to Child

	A	B	C	D	
101.	___	___	___	___	Shows interest/involvement in child's learning activities. Parent is not talking continuously, pays attention, and is listening.
102.	___	___	___	___	Is available when child asks for help, recognition, or sharing of activity.

2. Parent Participation in Child's Learning Activities.

      A   B   C   D

201. ____ ____ ____ ____   Helps to structure (set up) teacher assigned activity for the child so that child experiences it as meaningful and do-able.

202. ____ ____ ____ ____   Gives appropriate, facilitative, empowering help when child gets stuck (e.g., parent gives small clues which empower child) (vs. ignoring, criticizing, or belittling the child, or taking over the activity) (A3).

Empowering help means that the parent helps the child make the next step in the activity without doing it *for* the child. Parent gives child just enough help/hinting for the child to do it him/herself.

203. ____ ____ ____ ____   Constructively responds to child's mistakes by making suggestions, encouraging the child, or other constructive measures (vs. gets nervous/anxious, teases child about mistakes, scolds child for making mistakes, impatiently takes over the activity, etc.) (B1).

0 = No opportunity to observe this.
1 = Not present at all in parent's actions.
2 = Parent does not consistently give constructive responses but also does not take over activity.
3 = Fairly strong but fluctuating signs of parent constructively responding.
4 = Very strong and consistent signs of this in parent's actions. Caregiver also always gives encouragement and constructive suggestions.

204. ____ ____ ____ ____   Constructively verbalizes with child about the child's work, building language into the

activity (vs. fails to verbally interact with child around his/her learning activity) (C).

Rate this based on the opportunity for constructive verbalization. That is, whenever a teacher would be talking with a child about what the child is doing, commenting on their activities and progress, ask yourself, to what extent is the caregiver taking advantage of those opportunities?

0 = No opportunity to observe this.

1 = Not present at all in parent's actions. Parent never speaks to/with child about his/her activities.

2 = Slight signs of this. Parent only occasionally verbalizes with child.

3 = Parent verbalizes with child as teacher models activities. For example, parent repeats the colors with child during teacher quiz.

4 = Parent consistently initiates verbalization alone with child in separate activity. For example, parent tells child she sees the circle in her drawing.

206. ____ ____ ____ ____ Has age-appropriate expectations of child's learning level and performance (vs. gives child inappropriate tasks or gets upset and even intervenes when child does not perform up to some pre-set level).

207. ____ ____ ____ ____ Parent engages child's interest in free-play and is available for child and/or interactive with child during free play when appropriate.

208. ____ ____ ____ ____ Child completes home assignments.

3. Parent Giving Child Space to Do and Learn Things on His/Her Own

A   B   C   D

301. ____ ____ ____ ____ Gives child space to do things on his/her own (vs. crowds

child by pushing him/her,
intrudes on the child's activities unnecessarily, etc.) (A2).

302. ____ ____ ____ ____ Shows positive, valuing
response to child's explora-
tions, questions, inventiveness.

Positive response can be demonstrated "subtly" in a
smile or nod, as well as through more obvious demonstra-
tions and verbalizations.

303. ____ ____ ____ ____ Is process oriented rather than
product oriented in relating to
child's work.

1 = Very product oriented.
4 = Focuses predominantly on child's process of learning.
May praise child for good product or value it but does
not sacrifice process orientation to product orientation.

304. ____ ____ ____ ____ Remains patient with child
when child's learning goes
slowly or when child has
swings in mood or low energy
level.

1 = Frequently shows impatience.
2 = Mixture of patience and impatience.
3 = Usually shows patience but not totally consistent.
4 = Never shows impatience of this type. Maintains constant support when child is learning slowly or has swings
in mood or low energy level.

305. ____ ____ ____ ____ Does not derogatorily compare
child with other children.

1 = Frequently compares child derogatorily with other
children.
4 = Never compares child derogatorily with other children.

306. ____ ____ ____ ____ Does not engage with child
around learning activities in
ways which make the child nervous or regress (become self-
negating and less able to function).

1 = Frequently engages with child around learning activities in ways which make child nervous or regress.
4 = Never engages with child around learning activities in ways which make child nervous or regress.

4. Parent Positive Reinforcement of Child's Learning

      A   B   C   D

401. ____ ____ ____ ____   Shows positive response for product: shows positive response, praises child, for accomplishments big and small (vs. ignores or belittles child's success) (H1).

402. ____ ____ ____ ____   Shows positive response for process: shows positive response, praises child for trying, making efforts at learning (vs. ignores child's efforts or belittles them in some way) (I1).

0 = No chance to observe this.
1 = Not present at all in caretaker's actions. Caregiver ignores or belittles child's efforts.
2 = Does not praise child or show much positive response but also does not ignore child's efforts. Caregiver is ambivalent.
3 = Caregiver often praises/shows positive response to child for trying.
4 = Caregiver almost always praises/shows positive response to child for trying.

5. Parent in Relation to Child's Play

      A   B   C   D

501. ____ ____ ____ ____   Values child's play (vs. overly restricting, rejecting, critical, negating of child's play) (J1).

4 = Consistently does not control play. Allows the child to play on his/her own when appropriate.

502. ____ ____ ____ ____ Plays with child (is playful
with child) (vs. sees playful-
ness with child as inappropriate, a waste of time, too much
to bother with, etc.) (J2).

6. Parent Role in Child's Social Development

 A B C D

601. ____ ____ ____ ____ Takes responsibility for child's
disruptive behavior in class
(vs. ignores child's disruptive
behavior, fails to come to grips
with it).

602. ____ ____ ____ ____ Encourages child to share/take
turns.

7. Parent as Learner

 A B C D

701. ____ ____ ____ ____ Watches attentively as teacher
demonstrates or works with
child.

702. ____ ____ ____ ____ Makes effort to learn what children are being taught.
Parent pays sufficient attention to the teacher to learn the
relevant English words as well as enough attention to
understand *how to teach* child concepts.

8. Parent's Cooperation with the Class Process

 A B C D

803. ____ ____ ____ ____ Parent gets child to group on
time.

804. ____ ____ ____ ____ Parent consciously controls disruptive behavior of siblings or
others who might interfere
with child's learning.

805. ____ ____ ____ ____ Child comes to class appropriately dressed by CPS kindergar-
ten standards.

806. ＿＿ ＿＿ ＿＿ ＿＿ Child is not sleepy in class.

807. ＿＿ ＿＿ ＿＿ ＿＿ Child is not unusually hungry.

808. ＿＿ ＿＿ ＿＿ ＿＿ Child brings homework to class (reflecting parent investment and support in the homework process).

809. ＿＿ ＿＿ ＿＿ ＿＿ Parent shows interest in child borrowing books or in borrowing books for the child.

810. ＿＿ ＿＿ ＿＿ ＿＿ Child (or parent) returns borrowed books.

9. Child's Behavioral Indicators or Parent-Child Relationship

NOTE TO TEACHER: Each of the items in this last section assume that the parent is showing a particular kind of behavior and you are asked to rate the child's response. Item 903 assumes that parent sometimes doesn't come to class or leaves the child to work on his or her own so that the child's behavior under these conditions can be observed by the teacher. Item 904 assumes that the parent sometimes enters into the activity in a sharing (vs. dominant) collaborative way. If the parent never or virtually never shows the assumed behavior then put "NA" (not applicable). If the parent does show the assumed type of behavior but you have not had a chance to observe the child's response then put a "0" (i.e., not able to observe).

903. ＿＿ ＿＿ ＿＿ ＿＿ Child stays on task in caregiver's absence. 1 = Child cannot stay on task when caregiver not present, 4 = Child stays on task well in caregiver's absence.

904a. ＿＿ ＿＿ ＿＿ ＿＿ Child and caregiver capable of working in collaboration. Child does not withdraw when caregiver participates in the activity in a sharing (vs. dominating) manner, but rather works constructively as a partner with caregiver.

1 = Child withdraws completely when caregiver actively participates in doing the activity.

4 = Child does not withdraw when caregiver participates in the activity but rather holds his or her own and constructively collaborates with caregiver in doing the activity.

First and Second Grade Follow-Up Child Checklist*

Child's name _____

School _____

Grade _____

Teacher _____

Date checklist is filled out _____

Child has been in my class _____ months

Key to ratings on the checklist, unless otherwise indicated:

0 = No chance to observe this
1 = Not yet developing, no sign of it
2 = Beginning to be developed, initial signs of it at this time
3 = Moderately developed
4 = Well developed and very strong and consistent aspect of
   child's actions/capacities.

1. English Language/Social Uses

90. _____ How good is this child's English relative to the
   level of English that is necessary to function well
   in this classroom?

   1 = Not at all prepared.
   2 = Poorly prepared.
   3 = Moderately well/adequately prepared.
   4 = Very well prepared.

91. _____ What language(s) is (are) spoken in your classroom? (If it is not 100 percent English, give details
   to interviewer regarding what languages are used,
   in what proportion, by whom, in what contexts,
   etc.)

   _____

   _____

   _____

101. _____ How good is this child's language ability in
   English compared to a native English speaking
   child of the same age?

*Pre-K and Kindergarten Checklist is available upon request from Daniel R.
Scheinfeld, Erikson Institute, 420 North Wabash, Chicago, IL 60611.

1 = No apparent capacity in English.
2 = Beginning vocabulary with single words.
3 = Fairly developed capacity to understand and speak with single words and short phrases.
4 = Understands and speaks in whole sentences or understands most conversations with teacher and initiates English conversation.

102. _____ What is this child's attitude toward learning new words in English?
1 = Does not try.
2 = Tries a little.
3 = Tries quite a bit, but the trying fluctuates.
4 = Consistently tries to learn new words.

3. General Social-Emotional Development
301. _____ Social problem solving skills. For example, when there are too many children for a game or too many to fit at one table, child can work out a solution with his or her peers.
0 = No chance to observe this.
1 = Not yet developing, no sign of it.
2 = Beginning to be developed, initial signs of it at this time.
3 = Moderately developed.
4 = Well developed and very strong and consistent aspect of child's actions/capacities.

302. _____ Experience comfort around the teacher.

303. _____ Seeks out both adults and children for socializing.

304. _____ Expresses needs and feelings clearly to adults.

305. _____ Expresses feelings in a *socially acceptable way* (including angry or aggressive feelings).

306. _____ Self-esteem remains intact in the face of day-to-day disappointments.

4. Basic School Behaviors
401. _____ Follows simple verbal instructions, in English or native language (e.g., follows three-step directions).

0 = No chance to observe this.
1 = Not yet developing, no sign of it.
2 = Beginning to be developed, initial signs of it at this time.
3 = Moderately developed.
4 = Well developed and very strong and consistent aspect of child's actions/capacities.

402. _____ Able to sit and participate in a group.

403. _____ Can "line up" and function well in a lining up situation.

404. _____ Uses socially acceptable ways to gain attention.

405. _____ Seeks and uses teacher assistance when needed (can ask for help from the teacher).

406. _____ Approaches other children in a friendly way.

407. _____ Develops friendships with other children.

408. _____ Plays/works cooperatively with other children (e.g., when playing games or doing group activities).

409. _____ Gets along with children from his/her *own* ethnic group in a one-to-one or small group situation.
0 = No chance to observe this.
1 = Not yet developing, no sign of it.
2 = Beginning to be developed, initial signs of it at this time.
3 = Moderately developed.
4 = Well developed and very strong and consistent aspect of child's actions/capacities.

410. _____ Gets along with children from *other* ethnic groups in a one-to-one or small group situation.

411. _____ Respects other children's activities and personal property.

412. _____ Takes turns with other children (i.e., either voluntarily or when reminded).

413. _____ Shares toys and materials with other children.

414. _____ Respects the teacher's desk and belongings.

415. _____ Does not take home things that are the property of the classroom.

416. _____ Takes good care of classroom toys and materials.

417. _____ Puts things away after using them.

418. _____ Is able to clean up a small spill on his/her own without needing direction from the teacher.

419. _____ Responds with "please" and "thank you" appropriately.

420. _____ Uses eating utensils appropriately.

421. _____ Eats an adequate and varied meal at lunch.

5. Discipline and Order

500. _____ How well prepared was this child to follow the rules and regulations of the classroom when he/she arrived in your class, based on your expectations for a first/second grader?
   1 = Not at all prepared.
   2 = Poorly prepared.
   3 = Moderately well/adequately prepared.
   4 = Very well prepared.

501. _____ Comfortably follows classroom rules, routines, structure of the day.
   0 = No chance to observe this.
   1 = Not yet developing, no sign of it.
   2 = Beginning to be developed, initial signs of it at this time.
   3 = Moderately developed.
   4 = Well developed and very strong and consistent aspect of child's actions/capacities.

502. _____ Responds to teacher requests and directions (implies both understanding and being willing to respond). (Child listens attentively to adults.) (Responds to authority appropriately.)

503. _____ Accepts teacher limitations on activity without withdrawing or acting out.

6. Task Orientation

600. _____ How well prepared was this child to be task oriented when he/she arrived in your class, based on your expectations for a first/second grader?

1 = Not at all prepared.
2 = Poorly prepared.
3 = Moderately well/adequately prepared.
4 = Very well prepared.

601. _____ Works independently on assigned tasks for a reasonable length of time.

0 = No chance to observe this
1 = Not yet developing, no sign of it
2 = Beginning to be developed, initial signs of it at this time
3 = Moderately developed
4 = Well developed and very strong and consistent aspect of child's actions/capacities.

602. _____ Independently selects and engages in activities during free play or other times when choice is given.

0 = No chance to observe this
1 = Not yet developing, no sign of it
2 = Beginning to be developed, initial signs of it at this time
3 = Moderately developed
4 = Well developed and very strong and consistent aspect of child's actions/capacities.

603. _____ Initiates activities with other children, engages other children in play.

7. Tools, Motor Skills, and Materials of the Classroom

700. _____ How well prepared was this child to use pencil, paper, and other simple tools of the classroom when he/she arrived in your class, based on your expectations for a first/second grader?

1 = Not at all prepared.
2 = Poorly prepared.
3 = Moderately well/adequately prepared.
4 = Very well prepared.

701. _____ Uses pencil or pen

1 = Not at all
2 = By holding and using it with fist.
3 = By crudely holding it with finger and thumb but not yet very adept.
4 = By holding fairly or very adeptly with finger and thumb—comfortable, natural usage.

703. _____ Uses scissors with control to cut along wide, straight, and curved lines.
0 = No chance to observe this
1 = Not yet developing, no sign of it
2 = Beginning to be developed, initial signs of it at this time
3 = Moderately developed
4 = Well developed and very strong and consistent aspect of child's actions/capacities.

8. Motivated in School

800. _____ How well motivated to achieve in school was this child when he/she arrived in your class?
1 = Not at all motivated
2 = Motivated on rare occasions
3 = Motivated for a significant portion of the time
4 = Consistently motivated

801. _____ Shows interest and enthusiasm in learning activities.
0 = No chance to observe this
1 = Not yet developing, no sign of it
2 = Beginning to be developed, initial signs of it at this time
3 = Moderately developed
4 = Well developed and very strong and consistent aspect of child's actions/capacities.

802. _____ Shows pride in own accomplishments.

10. Self-management

1001. _____ Uses bathroom independently (toilet, washing hands, can pull down/up pants).
0 = No chance to observe this
1 = Not yet developing, no sign of it
2 = Beginning to be developed, initial signs of it at this time
3 = Moderately developed
4 = Well developed and very strong and consistent aspect of child's actions/capacities.

1002a. _____ Takes care of own personal belongings *with* direction from adults.

1002b. _____ Takes care of own personal belongings *without* direction from adults.

11. Hygiene

1100. _____ How well prepared was this child in his/her cleanliness habits when he/she arrived in your class based on your expectations for a first/second grader?

1 = Not at all prepared.
2 = Poorly prepared.
3 = Moderately well/adequately prepared.
4 = Very well prepared.

1101. _____ Is physically clean when comes to school (body, clothing)

0 = No chance to observe this
1 = Not yet developing, no sign of it
2 = Beginning to be developed, initial signs of it at this time
3 = Moderately developed
4 = Well developed and very strong and consistent aspect of child's actions/capacities.

1102. _____ Keeps hands and face clean during school.
1103. _____ General health level

1 = Very frequently ill and/or illnesses allowed to go untreated in ways that indicate insufficient caretaking.
2 = Fairly frequently ill
3 = Occasionally ill, normal
4 = Very seldom ill or not at all

12. Dress

1201. _____ Wears physically appropriate clothing for weather conditions.

0 = No chance to observe this
1 = Not yet developing, no sign of it
2 = Beginning to be developed, initial signs of it at this time
3 = Moderately developed
4 = Well developed and very strong and consistent aspect of child's actions/capacities.

13. Attendance

1301. _____ Attendance at school

1 = Very poor attendance; 30 percent or less
2 = Fairly poor attendance; 30–60 percent
3 = Fairly regular but not entirely stable; 60–80 percent
4 = Good stable attendance; 85–100 percent

14. Parental Involvement

Key to Ratings on Parent Involvement

0 = No chance to observe this
1 = Not yet developing, no sign of it
2 = Beginning to be developed, initial signs of it at this time
3 = Partially developed but fluctuates
4 = Well developed and very strong and consistent aspect of parent's actions/capacities.

1401. _____ Child gets to school on time

1402. _____ Picks up the child or has the child picked up from school on time.

1403. _____ Attends requested conferences with the teacher

1404. _____ Attends parent group meetings

1405. _____ Seems to be comfortable with the teacher.

1406. _____ Seems to be comfortable with bilingual worker.

1407. _____ Helps with the class

1408. _____ Shows concern for the child
1 = Seems disconnected, disinterested in the child
2 = Shows occasional, sporadic interested but the concern is heavily compromised by other considerations or general low interest
3 = Shows fairly consistent concern for the child, but can fluctuate at times
4 = Shows steady, nurturing concern for the child

1409. _____ Responsive in some appropriate way(s) to letters and announcements sent home with the child or by mail.
0 = No chance to observe this
1 = Not yet developing, no sign of it
2 = Beginning to be developed, initial signs of it at this time
3 = Moderately developed
4 = Well developed and very strong and consistent aspect of parent's actions/capacities.

1410. _____ Is attendant to the child's health needs

1411. _____ Helps with and supports child's homework activities. Parent is interactive and supportive with respect to these activities, but does not do the child's homework for him/her.

1490. _____ Overall willingness of parent(s) to act as a partner with the teacher in respect to the child's education

0 = No chance to observe this
1 = Not yet developing, no sign of it
2 = Beginning to be developed, initial signs of it at this time
3 = Moderately developed
4 = Well developed and very strong and consistent aspect of parent's actions/capacities.

15. Language Arts—Based on your knowledge of national norms for children in this grade, *at this time of year.*
(For first and second grade)

1500. _____ How well does this child visually recognize words and their meanings?

4 = Performing *above* grade level, for this time of year, based on national norms.
3 = Performing *at* grade level, for this time of year, based on national norms.
2 = Performing *up to a year below* grade level for this time of year, based on national norms.
1 = Performing *more than a year below* grade level, for this time of year, based on national norms.

1501. _____ Where would you say this child is in his/her current ability to sound out new words?

4 = Performing *above* grade level, for this time of year, based on national norms.
3 = Performing *at* grade level, for this time of year, based on national norms.
2 = Performing *up to a year below* grade level for this time of year, based on national norms.
1 = Performing *more than a year below* grade level, for this time of year, based on national norms.

1502. _____ Where would you say this child is in his/her current ability to comprehend a story that is read by the teacher?

4 = Performing *above* grade level, for this time of year, based on national norms.
3 = Performing *at* grade level, for this time of year, based on national norms.
2 = Performing *up to a year below* grade level for this time of year, based on national norms.
1 = Performing *more than a year below* grade level, for this time of year, based on national norms.

(Item 1503 for second grade only)

1503. _____ Where would you say this child is in his/her *reading* comprehension?
4 = Performing *above* grade level, for this time of year, based on national norms.
3 = Performing *at* grade level, for this time of year, based on national norms.
2 = Performing *up to a year below* grade level for this time of year, based on national norms.
1 = Performing *more than a year below* grade level, for this time of year, based on national norms.

(For first and second graders)

16. Math—Based on your knowledge of national norms for children in this grade, *at this time of year.*
1600. _____ Where would you say this child is in his/her current ability in math?
4 = Performing *above* grade level, for this time of year, based on national norms.
3 = Performing *at* grade level, for this time of year, based on national norms.
2 = Performing *up to a year below* grade level for this time of year, based on national norms.
1 = Performing *more than a year below* grade level, for this time of year, based on national norms.

_ _

Teacher and Interviewer Sort Index Cards for Class Ranking
Please rank all the children in your classroom into categories of 1 = below average; 2 = average; 3 = above average; in each of the major categories listed in this card.

4" × 6" Sorting Cards for the School Performance Sorting Task Follow-Up Study

Preschool and Kindergarten Child Rating Card—Side 1

Name of child: _____

Ethnicity: _____   Birthdate: ____/____/____

Caregiver: _____   Cycle(s)–Groups(s): _____

_____

Exit date: ____/____/____   Time in Groups: _____

Started School   School: _____

Date: ____/____/____

Grade: _____

Preschool and Kindergarten Child Rating Card—Side 2

Child ID No.: _____   School code: _____

Teacher ID No.: _____   Grade: _____

Category	Rank	Category	Rank
1. English language	____	8. Motivated	____
2. Conceptual development	____	9. Gross motor	____
3. Social-emotional development	____	10. Self-management	____
4. School behavior	____	11. Hygiene	____
5. Discipline/order	____	12. Dress	____
6. Task orientation	____	13. Attendance	____
7. Motor skills	____	14. Parent involved	____

Comments:

First and Second Grade Follow-Up Rating Card—Side 1

Name of child: _____

Ethnicity: _____   Birthdate: ____/____/____

Caregiver: _____   Cycle(s)–Groups(s): _____

_____

Exit date: ____/____/____   Time in Groups: _____

Started School   School: _____

Date: ____/____/____

Grade: _____

First and Second Grade Follow-Up Rating Card—Side 2

Child ID No.: _____   School code: _____

Teacher ID No.: _____   Grade: _____

Category	Rank	Category	Rank
1. English language	____	10. Self-management	____
3. Social-emotional development	____	11. Hygiene	____
4. School behavior	____	12. Dress	____
5. Discipline/order	____	13. Attendance	____
6. Task orientation	____	14. Parent involved	____
7. Motor skills	____	15. Language arts	____
8. Motivated	____	16. Math	____

References

Board of Education of the City of Chicago. Child Assessment Profile for Early Childhood Programs: Handbook for Teachers, Chicago Public Schools. Board of Education of the City of Chicago, Chicago, 1989.

Escobar, L. E., and McKeon, R. Adult Basic Education TESOL Handook. Edited by Diana Hartley. Collier McMillan, 1979.

Kaplan, L. Working with Multiproblem Families. Lexington Books, Lexington, Mass., 1986.

Langendorf, T., and Koch, V. Refugee Families Program Report, 13 January 1995. (The cited quote is edited from the original.)

Linacre, J. M., and Wright, B. D. The User's Guide to Big Steps: Rasch Model Computer Program. Mesa Press, Chicago, 1993.